Second Edition

BOWLING
e**X**ecution

Second Edition

BOWLING eXecution

John Jowdy

Human Kinetics

Library of Congress Cataloging-in-Publication Data

Jowdy, John, 1920-
  Bowling execution / John Jowdy. -- 2nd ed.
    p. cm.
  Includes index.
  ISBN-13: 978-0-7360-7538-1 (soft cover)
  ISBN-10: 0-7360-7538-0 (soft cover)
  1. Bowling. 2. Bowling. I. Title.
  GV903.J69 2009
  794.6--dc22

                          2008046877

ISBN-10: 0-7360-7538-0 (print)   ISBN-10: 0-7360-8482-7 (Adobe PDF)
ISBN-13: 978-0-7360-7538-1 (print)   ISBN-13: 978-0-7360-8482-6 (Adobe PDF)

The Web addresses cited in this text were current as of December 2008, unless otherwise noted.

Acquisitions Editor: Justin Klug; **Developmental Editor:** Cynthia McEntire; **Assistant Editor:** Scott Hawkins; **Copyeditor:** Tom Tiller; **Proofreader:** John Wentworth; **Indexer:** Dan Connolly; **Permission Manager:** Martha Gullo; **Graphic Designer:** Joe Buck; **Graphic Artist:** Tara Welsch; **Cover Designer:** Keith Blomberg; **Photographer (cover):** Neil Bernstein; **Photographer (interior):** Neil Bernstein, unless otherwise noted; **Visual Production Assistant:** Joyce Brumfield; **Photo Office Assistant:** Jason Allen; **Art Manager:** Kelly Hendren; **Illustrators:** Alan L. Wilborn and Roberto Sabas; **Printer:** Hess Print Solutions

We thank North Rock Lanes in Wichita, Kansas, for assistance in providing the location for the photo shoot for this book.

Human Kinetics books are available at special discounts for bulk purchase. Special editions or book excerpts can also be created to specification. For details, contact the Special Sales Manager at Human Kinetics.

Printed in the United States of America   10 9 8 7 6 5 4 3 2 1

Human Kinetics
Web site: www.HumanKinetics.com

United States: Human Kinetics
P.O. Box 5076
Champaign, IL 61825-5076
800-747-4457
e-mail: humank@hkusa.com

Canada: Human Kinetics
475 Devonshire Road Unit 100
Windsor, ON N8Y 2L5
800-465-7301 (in Canada only)
e-mail: info@hkcanada.com

Europe: Human Kinetics
107 Bradford Road
Stanningley
Leeds LS28 6AT, United Kingdom
+44 (0) 113 255 5665
e-mail: hk@hkeurope.com

Australia: Human Kinetics
57A Price Avenue
Lower Mitcham, South Australia 5062
08 8372 0999
e-mail: info@hkaustralia.com

New Zealand: Human Kinetics
Division of Sports Distributors NZ Ltd.
P.O. Box 300 226 Albany
North Shore City
Auckland
0064 9 448 1207
e-mail: info@humankinetics.co.nz

I dedicate this book to my wife, Brenda: my best friend, my editor, my inspiration, and the love of my life. She contributed as much as I did, if not more, to making this book a reality. Her contributions were invaluable.

Contents

Foreword

In every sport there are many great coaches. But there are only a select few that you can call "outstanding." However, in the sport of bowling John Jowdy certainly defines OUTSTANDING. He has a special eye for seeing the intricate details that can take your ability from an average bowler, to one who can compete on a week to week basis amongst the best in the world. I feel extremely fortunate to have crossed paths with him in the mid 1980's and honored to have had him as one of my extra set of eyes. He by far, through his wealth of knowledge, has helped take my career of rolling a bowling ball to be one of the best in the world.

To look at John, he is man with a 12 inch stogie and you could easily mistake him for a fan coming in for a cup of coffee. And what could he possibly know about timing and techniques. Let me tell you, his expertise in the sport of bowling exceeds the depth of the Grand Canyon and is as long as the Mississippi River. A gentle man with the utmost respect amongst all the great professionals, John could help the player who is about to throw in the towel to be on the next telecast if you are willing. It is amazing how his presence on a given week on tour can find one of his students competing for the title.

If you have an open mind and are willing to put in the time necessary on the lanes, I am confident that the book you are about to read will take your game further than you thought your dreams could. John possesses a wide range of ability to help ALL bowlers. Regardless of average or what hand you deliver it with, I guarantee you will increase your overall knowledge of the game with what you are about to read. Putting John's extraordinary teaching abilities aside, I can't think of a better coach than this man to help you take your game for the ride of a lifetime.

If you add up the numbers throughout his tenure, Mr. Jowdy certainly leads two distinct categories: All-Time Titles as well as All-Time Earnings, by a long shot. There is not another coach in the 50 year history of the

PBA who measures up to these accomplishments. We will see the fruits of his labor for many, many years to come.

I encourage you to sit back, relax and take in what you are about to read. This PBA and USBC Hall of Famer is one of the greatest coaches who have ever laid eyes on the lanes.

Parker Bohn III.

PBA Player of the Year, 1999, 2001-02
Winner of 31 PBA titles

Preface

During the past six years, many changes have occurred that have affected bowling. First of all the governing bodies of the game, the American Bowling Congress (ABC), the Women's International Bowling Congress (WIBC), and the Young American Bowling Alliance merged into one governing group called the United States Bowling Congress (USBC).

After several years of servicing bowling from their Milwaukee headquarters, the USBC agreed to accept an offer from the Bowling Proprietors of America (BPA) to move to Arlington, Texas, where communications between them would become more advantageous in consolidating the principal integers of bowling. In addition to this, the International Bowling Hall of Fame and Museum also agreed to move from St. Louis to help form a great bowling complex in the very popular tourist attraction area of Six Flags Over Texas.

In another constructive move, the BPA, under the astute direction of executive director John Berglund, took over operations of the International Bowling Pro Shop Instruction Association (IBPSIA), the standard of excellence in the operation of bowling pro shops around the world.

Since the publication of the first edition of *Bowling Execution,* a major change was instituted in the PBA format. The field of entries was limited to 64 exempt players. Exempt status was based on a point system, a limit in the number of entries that would make up the regular pro tour.

Unfortunately, this change ended the careers of several stars who either failed to qualify in the point list or, in many cases, chose to retire from the pro ranks and return home to greener pastures in the bowling industry. Among those who chose to retire from the regular pro tour were Mike Aulby, Dave Husted, Roger Bowker, Eric Forkel, Bryan Goebel, Steve Hoskins, Bob Learn, Mark Roth, Rick Steelsmith, Brian Voss, and Rickey Ward. These players were replaced by newcomers such as Patrick Allen, Richie Allen, Mike Devaney, Michael Fagan, Michael Haugen, Tommy Jones, Wes Malott, Bill O'Neill, Sean Rash, Tony Reyes, and Mike Wolfe.

Additionally, this era in bowling signaled the end of the Ladies Professional Bowling Tour (LPBT). The tour lost its TV contract and, despite efforts by the WIBC to revive it, it was dissolved. Nonetheless, the Professional Bowlers Association (PBA) opened its doors to all female performers. Taking advantage of this opportunity, 23 ladies joined the PBA, including former regular members of the LPBT, Carolyn Dorin-Ballard, Kelly Kulick, and Liz Johnson.

Kulick made history when she qualified for the 64 exempt tour by bowling her way through the tour trials. Although Liz Johnson never succeeded in qualifying through the tour trials, she did quite well in the weekly pro tour qualifying rounds. Liz became the first female to advance not only to the national TV finals but to the title match by defeating Wes Malott 235-228. She lost her match against Tommy Jones, 219-192.

Countless books have been published regarding proper bowling techniques. While many are informative and technically beneficial for an aspiring bowler, none offers a more in-depth look at the finer points of the sport than *Bowling Execution*. This book will help you make sense of everything you have learned before this. The principles behind a well-executed shot will finally be easy to implement. You will gain a greater understanding of the intricacies of the game learn how to apply this information to consistently generate quality shots under any conditions.

My suggestions are based on modern principles and techniques that have been tested and proven on the PBA tour. This book is directed to serious bowlers who prefer to compete on conditions that demand quality shots; it is not for bowlers who remain content in posting unrealistic averages on blocked lanes.

Acknowledgments

If my bowling knowledge, experience, and talents have earned me the privilege of writing this book, I want to thank those who were instrumental in my development and success as a coach and writer.

First and foremost, I would like to thank the Columbia 300 bowling ball family. I have been associated with this company for more than 40 years, and it was Columbia that afforded me the opportunity to attend tournaments (professional as well as amateur) throughout the United States and other areas of the world. Particularly, I want to thank the late founders of the company—Mr. and Mrs. Roger Zeller and Mr. Zeller's successor, Ronald Herrmann—for their support and friendship. The management that guided my path at Columbia included Pepper Martin, John Rizzo, and Mike Allbritton.

In February 2007, Ebonite International acquired the assets of Columbia 300. Bill Scheid, CEO of Ebonite, offered me the opportunity to continue my association with Columbia 300, and I am pleased to say that I currently enjoy the same family atmosphere with Bill Scheid, as well as with president of marketing Bob Reid and Columbia 300 brand manager Chad Murphy.

Three of the most noted bowling writers in the United States—Dick Evans, Joe Lyou, and Chuck Pezzano—deserve recognition for their encouraging words and insightful tips, as well as their friendship.

My deep appreciation goes to PBA commissioner Fred Schreyer and the PBA staff, particularly Kirk Von Krueger and Janay Leddy for their wholehearted support in arranging photo shoots of the world's greatest bowlers and full cooperation in other matters so pertinent to the development of this book. Thank you to Frank and Kathy Desocia, proprietors of North Rock Lanes, for affording us the facilities for the photo shoot.

Tom Kouros, author of *Par Bowling*, and, in my opinion, the most knowledgeable individual in bowling, has my sincere thanks for volunteering vital material, thereby making this book more informative.

Other generous contributors to this book who get my thanks are Mark Miller and Bill Vint of the United States Bowling Congress. My special thanks to Jerry Francomano for sharing his expertise on measuring and fitting bowling balls. Special thanks to Columbia 300's Danny Speranza for his keen insight regarding the structure of bowling balls—how they react and the effect they have on the lanes.

Thanks to my good friend Rolf Gauger, one of America's topflight instructors, for his input and support in making this book possible.

I want to express my sincere gratitude to all of the Professional Bowling Association bowlers who contributed their time to make this book more interesting, including Patrick Allen, Tom Baker, Chris Barnes, Jason Bellmonte, Parker Bohn III, Michael Haugen Jr., Steve Jaros, Tommy Jones, Doug Kent, Tim Mack, Wes Mallot, Sean Rash, Robert Smith, Pete Weber, Walter Ray Williams, and Danny Wiseman. I also want to express appreciation to Brenda Mack and Clara Guerrero who contributed their time and efforts.

Last, but not least, I'd like to thank everyone at Human Kinetics, particularly Cynthia McEntire and Justin Klug, for their patience, guidance, and assistance in making this assignment an easier endeavor—and a most enjoyable one.

Visualizing Success

Physical talent is the primary requirement for any athlete. In bowling, however, physical talent alone is not enough. Thousands of bowlers possess outstanding physical talent but never reach the heights for which they aim. Countless amateur bowlers with incredible physical games, many averaging over 220, flounder and seem lost when faced with challenges in unfamiliar territory. Ever-changing lane conditions—such as dry heads, oil carry-down, changing breakpoints, excessive oil in favored zones, and other variables in lane maintenance—can confuse and humble even the best, regardless of their talent. This bewilderment is compounded when bowlers leave familiar house conditions for tournaments.

Such circumstances also fluster many top-rated pros. The reason for this perplexity is bowlers' failure to recognize the importance of developing the mental dimension of their game. Herein lies the disparity between, on one hand, amateurs and less successful pros, and, on the other hand, those who earn a living in the ranks of professional bowling. Even as you learn the basics of the physical aspect of bowling, you need to understand the importance of the mental aspect. This dual approach is discussed, for example, in chapter 8, where it is addressed in the context of establishing a preshot comfort zone, which requires both physical and mental components of relaxation. The point is that no matter what part of the physical game we are talking about, the mental aspect is right there begging for our attention.

I strongly recommend reading Dean Hinitz's *Focused for Bowling* (Human Kinetics, 2003), the most comprehensive book on the mental aspect of the game. Dr. Dean is the preeminent sport psychologist working with today's top-rated bowlers (male and female). He is a member of the Team USA coaching staff and conducts bowling clinics in numerous college programs. He is also a member of several private bowling clinics throughout the country.

Because the mental approach to bowling is so important, it seems appropriate to begin by clearly identifying some aspects of the mental game. Then, as you move through this book, it will become second nature for you to address both the physical and the mental aspects of the game.

Many top amateurs in the country have tested the waters on the PBA Tour. Many have succeeded, but the majority have returned to the greener pastures and easier pickings of the higher scores and the cash to be found in megabucks tournaments and other amateur events. There is, however, a price to pay. Although the huge prize funds are tempting, megabucks promoters do not permit former PBA members to compete if they have won a national title. Consequently, bowlers are faced with a difficult choice: an opportunity to bowl for a huge sum of money against weaker competition or the distinction of a PBA title against the world's best players. Winning a title is the goal of every PBA player. Given a choice between the money and a title, a professional bowler would prefer the title every time, and every bowler wants to know the magic formula for winning. Again, the answer is a combination of physical talent *and* mental ability.

Bowling is a totally offensive game; it has no defensive position. As with golf, it depends entirely on individual performance, and the deciding factor between bowlers of equal ability is the mental state of the participants.

So, what constitutes a sound mental game, one that distinguishes winners from also-rans? The answer can be broken down into these basic qualities: awareness and intelligence, concentration, and confidence. (Two other aspects of mental focus are reading the lanes, covered in chapter 2, and understanding the equipment, discussed in chapter 11.)

Awareness and Intelligence

Awesome physical strength can sometimes be beneficial, but the better bowler will play to the demands of the lanes and deliver accordingly. It is your choice—a matter of brains versus brawn. One principle remains steadfast: No matter how great the bowler may be, lane conditions prescribe the proper attack for scoring. This must be your paramount thought. You take what the lanes permit. You cannot overcome lane conditions on a consistent basis unless you adjust to them. You may get away with one or two deliveries that are not conducive to the conditions at hand, but, as a general rule, you will ultimately fail. You must be aware of the lane conditions and use your bowling intelligence to adapt.

Unfortunately, many aspiring bowlers believe that excessive revolutions provide the answer to successful execution. They revel at the sight of the ball crossing 10 to 18 boards in a wide-arcing trajectory, then booming back off the second or third board at the breakpoint and splattering pins in all directions. I refer to this as a Hollywood shot. The strikes are exciting, but this is the toughest path to success. This type of delivery is reminiscent of golfers who smash uncontrollable drives in excess of 300 yards (275 meters) yet finish strokes behind those who control 235- to 250-yard (215- to 230-meter) tee shots.

In bowling, there is some value to the old adage that "the shortest distance between two points is a straight line." This is not to suggest that a straight ball in bowling is superior to a hook; it merely indicates that an effective hook is one with sufficient drive to carry the 5-pin. The defining word here is *control*. Short hooks are easier to control and have a higher carrying percentage. They are also less likely to produce difficult spare shots.

Concentration

Concentration is the ability to focus on the subject at hand. In bowling, the prime objective is to put the ball in the pocket. This must be uppermost in your thought process. Elite bowlers concentrate on the job at hand by means of methods including distraction control, breath control, self-talk, and preshot routines.

Many observers, including Hall of Famer Johnny Petraglia and former PBA tournament director Harry Golden, consider Don Johnson to be the greatest clutch bowler they've ever seen. Johnson admitted that he was far less talented than most of his competitors, yet he managed to win 26 PBA titles before injuries forced him into retirement. His focus was so intense that he was oblivious to sounds and other distractions that would have rattled average bowlers, especially in crucial situations. His ability to manage distractions led to his success.

Danny Wiseman's focus and accuracy have helped him become a successful pro.

Mike Aulby also demonstrated the trait of utter concentration. One of the most disciplined bowlers in history, Aulby could be matched or surpassed in ability by numerous players. Nevertheless, he is the only player to date who has captured all five major titles: the PBA National, the Touring Players Championship, the U.S. Open, the Tournament of Champions, and the ABC Masters. He is also the only player to have won the coveted ABC Masters three times. One of his shining moments came in 1995, when he completed the Triple Crown cycle by winning the Tournament of Champions in the way he so often did—striking out in the 10th frame when all three strikes were needed. This performance provided further evidence of Aulby's extraordinary mental toughness.

Amleto Monacelli has recorded 18 titles in his career. With all due respect to his tremendous talent, Amleto's cerebral approach to the game has been one of his greatest assets. Amleto was the top seed at the 1988 Showboat Invitational, televised on ABC in an era when PBA telecasts were producing unusually low scores. PBA lane maintenance staff were flabbergasted at their inability to overcome the problem of lighting effects on oil patterns. On this particular day, the scores of the first three matches were embarrassingly low. The oil carry-down made it virtually impossible to hit the pocket with any consistency, and strikes were almost nonexistent. In fact, Monacelli, whose forte is a powerful hook, was bewildered during the first five frames. His hook ball was ineffective, either overreacting or simply skidding. His opponent was equally puzzled. At the end of the fifth frame, with both players struggling and the game fairly even, Monacelli displayed his mental prowess by reverting to a straight shot, direct to the pocket. Although strikes were still not to be found, Amleto managed high counts and easy spares. He endured and emerged victorious with, believe it or not, a 158 game! It was not pretty, but it was good enough to cart off a title.

So what can you do to achieve the level of concentration that successful pros bring to the table? One of my favorite suggestions for transforming concentration is to draw a picture in your mind, wherein your strike shot enters the pocket and demolishes the pins. This is the power of positive thinking. Think positively, and your results are more likely to be positive. Also, as you are seated and awaiting your turn to bowl, recall your successes and how you accomplished them. More important, think of how you felt, and cultivate the same feeling you had at that time. All of these suggestions are based on positive thinking—the most basic element of concentration and confidence.

Here are some additional tips from two members of the former Ladies Professional Bowlers Tour who have exhibited great powers of concentration:

1. Treat each shot the same, focusing on execution rather than outcome.

I try not to treat one shot any differently from another but rather focus on making the best shot I can each and every time; by doing so, you focus on execution rather than outcome. Chances are that if you execute well, the score will take care of itself.

Cara Honeychurch
2000 Professional Women's Bowling Association (PWBA) Rookie of the Year

2. Relax and stay positive.

I clear my mind of negative thoughts in crucial situations. I try to stay as positive as possible. Sometimes it's hard, but I have a few things I repeat over and over to myself to help me relax and keep positive. On TV, I always make sure to breathe a lot. This helps me to relax and helps me maintain my focus.

Carolyn Dorin-Ballard
2000 PWBA Player of the Year runner-up

3. Don't get mad; get even.

Bowling made its first appearance in the Commonwealth Games in Malaysia in 1998. The Commonwealth Games are similar to the Olympics but for Commonwealth countries only. Malaysia had a strong team and was expected to do well; however, they had targeted me as the biggest threat to their success and decided to resort to alternative tactics to distract me. This campaign was called Operation Cara and included such things as the media writing unfavorable things about me in the newspapers and people blowing horns and making other loud noises during my approach. None of these people were reprimanded or asked to leave the venue. As you can imagine, it took a great deal of concentration and belief in myself to be able to overcome such trying circumstances. However, I was able to do so, and this resulted in my winning three gold medals. It will always go down in my mind as one of my greatest achievements.

Cara Honeychurch

4. Take it game by game.

My husband, Del Ballard, has influenced me the most in dealing with my mental game. He taught me how to approach a tournament each week, game by game, not day by day. I used to always think ahead and get lost in the shuffle. He taught me that you cannot win a tournament during the qualification rounds; you win in head-to-head competition. Putting things in perspective allowed me to focus in the right direction.

Carolyn Dorin-Ballard

Confidence

Confidence consists of faith in one's ability to perform in clutch situations. Norm Duke has risen to superstar status not only by virtue of his incredible talent but also through his bowling intellect. His thought process, his compliance with lane dictates, and his confidence in the way he attacks the lanes have set him apart from those who lack his mental approach.

Chris Barnes was one of the best amateur bowlers in the world before joining the PBA Tour, where he became an instant success. His greatest assets are his intellectual method of operation and his supreme confidence. His knack for reading lanes and willingness to conform to lane dictates, combined with his magical hand, account for his status as one of the top stars on the Tour.

Chris Barnes's confidence and intense concentration give him an edge over his competitors.

Talent and lane savvy speak for themselves as keys to success, and success breeds confidence. The world is replete with egotists who exude false confidence. They hustle easy pickings and are usually backed by others. Free of real pressure, they freewheel and bask in undeserved glory.

In contrast, true confidence involves the ability to quietly apply pressure to opponents, as Don Carter and Earl Anthony did during their brilliant careers. Both caused other bowlers to look over their shoulder as they anticipated the inevitable charge. Their many appearances in championship matches gave them a psychological advantage. They were a study in concentration and could not be counted out until it was mathematically impossible for them to win. They seldom missed the opportunity to jump on an opponent's mistake and were a virtual cinch to strike out if an opponent left an opening late in the game. The same can be said of current PBA stars Norm Duke and Walter Ray Williams.

Carolyn Dorin-Ballard possesses the same demeanor that Carter and Anthony did. Although very personable and a friend to everyone off the lanes, she approaches the game with supreme confidence and concentration. On the lanes, Carolyn Dorin-Ballard is all business!

Superstars such as Dick Weber, Don Johnson, and Mark Roth are set apart from other bowlers by their confidence. Weber's warm personality belied his fierce competitiveness. He spoke kindly, smiled, showed appreciation for an opponent's success, acted as the perfect gentleman, and then battered his opponents with a barrage of strikes. He beat them to a pulp and still made them love him.

Johnson was a real pro. He got more out of his game than any bowler in history. He had the guts of a gorilla and made the most radical moves that anyone could imagine. On numerous occasions, Johnson would abandon a deep inside line in favor of an area outside the 5th board, ever confident and never flinching.

Mark Roth, another immortal, turned in one of the greatest demonstrations of confidence I have ever seen. It was 1977, and the place was Norwalk, California, where Roth faced hometown favorite Bobby Fliegman in a televised title match. Roth stepped up in the 10th frame needing three strikes to win by a pin. Mark was forced to finish his 10th frame on a lane where he hadn't come remotely close to striking in four previous tries. He uncorked three perfect strikes to take the match. Roth exuded knowledge, concentration, and confidence—ingredients that constitute proper mental preparation.

So how can you build and maintain the level of confidence enjoyed by these successful pros? And when you lose confidence in your game, how can you rebuild it? Here are a few suggestions from the pros:

Like Carolyn Dorin-Ballard, Brenda Mack approaches the game with supreme confidence and concentration.

1. Identify problems in your game and strive to fix them.

The more I learn about something from every angle, the more confidence I have. Usually if you think you have problems with your game physically, it is really something mental. And if you are mentally confused with your game, concentrate on the physical game because there's usually something wrong there. Have fun, set new goals, realize it is a time of renewal and change. Go with the flow; do not fight it, just go with it.

Kim Adler
Top PWBA pro with 14 titles

2. Get back on track with changes you believe in.

When you lose confidence in your performances, you have to make changes . . . changes that will put you back on track. You not only make changes . . . you have to have faith in the changes in order to regain confidence.

Marshall Holman
PBA Hall of Famer

3. Recall instances when you successfully overcame a difficult situation.

If I have lost my confidence, there is usually a reason for it, and so the first thing I do is identify what part of my game is suffering and attempt to rectify the issue. Confidence is a state of mind and takes time to build. If I feel that I am lacking confidence, I will think of all the situations throughout my bowling career where I have triumphed in challenging circumstances and what I did to overcome those difficulties.

Cara Honeychurch

4. Review tapes of yourself bowling at your best or consult with a coach.

If I start to lose confidence, I watch a lot of my TV shows. Especially those in which I feel I was bowling my best. I also bowl everything I can during this time to get that one great tournament, or block, or an overall feeling that things are getting better. Confidence is all in how you feel about yourself.

Carolyn Dorin-Ballard

5. Take pride in your accomplishments. Don't dwell on mistakes.

I have been Player of the Year runner-up for four years. Although I have learned to take great pride in this accomplishment, the last few years had me looking at what I might be lacking to achieve this goal. I have to take pride in what I achieve, not dwell on what I do not accomplish. If you take pride and joy in what you do well, this is a great foundation for self-confidence.

Carolyn Dorin-Ballard

Successful bowlers demonstrate more than raw physical talent. They are able to adjust mentally to lane and game conditions, eliminate distractions, approach the lanes with confidence, and visualize success. A positive mental approach on the lane creates more confidence and leads to consistently higher scores.

Reading and Adapting to the Lanes

As discussed in chapter 1, half of a bowler's mental game is made up of awareness, intelligence, concentration, and confidence. Equally important is the ability to read lanes and conform to what the lane dictates.

Amateur and league bowlers are accustomed to lanes conditioned for high scores. Though it may not be the case everywhere, most proprietors cater to customers who derive pleasure from posting high averages. This is not meant as an indictment of proprietors who want to please their clientele; it is simply an attempt to stress the simplicity of house conditions as compared with those on the PBA Tour and those of megabucks events.

In the early days of bowling, oil conditioner was applied to the lane as a barrier to protect the surface from damage over years of use. Oil became part of the sport, as lacquer, polyurethane, and other synthetic surfaces became more popular. Today, PBA bowlers must adjust their strategies and methods when attacking the challenging conditions of the lanes, and PBA Experience leagues give amateur bowlers the opportunity to compete on the five lane-conditioning patterns used in PBA tournaments: Chameleon, Cheetah, Scorpion, Shark, and Viper (figure 2.1).

Chameleon measures 39 feet (11.9 meters) in oil distance and constitutes a retro approach to pattern design. Oil is placed in strips, which requires a bowler to play in a specific zone on the lane; this pattern contrasts sharply with a multiple-angles condition. The scoring pace for this pattern can range from low to high, depending on the condition of the surface.

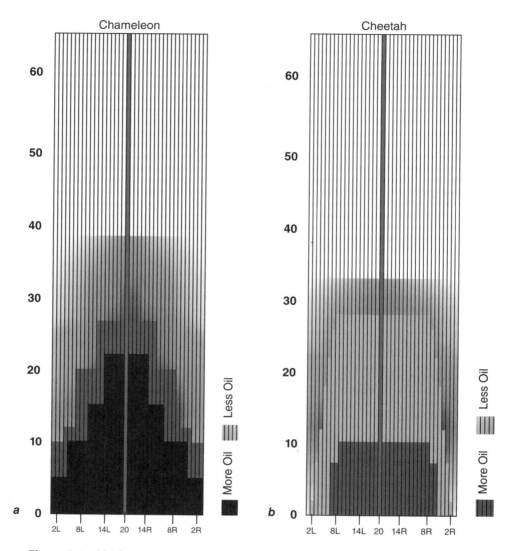

Figure 2.1 PBA lane-conditioning patterns: *(a)* Chameleon, *(b)* Cheetah, *(c)* Scorpion, *(d)* Shark, *(e)* Viper.

Cheetah, the shortest of the five patterns, measures 35 feet (10.7 meters). Sometimes applied on well-worn lane surfaces, Cheetah maximizes use of areas in the lane that are less worn (usually areas extremely close to the gutter). As a result, players tend to migrate toward those spots to take advantage of the more pristine surface. Cheetah is exciting because it allows players to make risk–reward decisions based on playing near the gutter. Scoring pace for this pattern is usually medium to high.

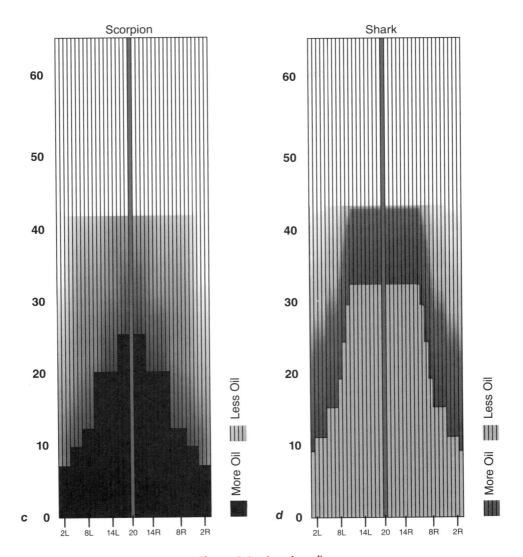

Figure 2.1 *(continued).*

Scorpion measures 41 feet (12.5 meters). As with Viper, it allows a wide variety of attack strategies depending on the type and condition of the lane surface. However, Scorpion incorporates a larger volume of oil farther down the lane, which often requires a more direct line. Scoring pace is usually low to medium for this pattern.

Shark, the longest of the five patterns, measures 44 feet (13.4 meters). Bowlers tend to migrate more toward the center of the lane, since the ball

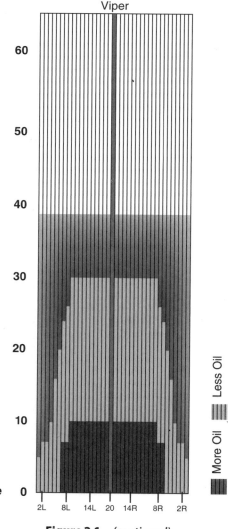

Figure 2.1 *(continued)*.

usually will not hook back to the pocket if it strays too far toward the gutter. After five or six games, bowlers often find that this pattern requires extreme inside angles to get to the pocket. Scoring pace is usually high for this pattern.

Viper measures 37 feet (11.3 meters) in oil distance. More than any other oil pattern, Viper allows a wide variety of attack strategies, depending on the type and condition of the lane surface. Scoring pace is usually medium to high for this pattern.

Testing the Lane

Reading lanes is probably the most difficult task that bowlers face. Oil patterns are not detectable by the naked eye; oil is colorless, and seeking a line to the pocket is like running an obstacle course while blindfolded. In golf, hazards such as sand traps, high grass, trees, and water are clearly visible, but bowlers are not afforded this luxury. Bowlers have to speculate and take risks based on unseen obstacles.

Changing oil patterns result primarily from increased activity in certain playing areas. Urethane balls designed to create greater friction wreak havoc on lane conditioning, and advances such as reactive resin and proactive coverstocks have further complicated oil patterns. Although these new tools have been a boon to players who throw harder and straighter shots, they have further complicated the process of choosing proper equipment. In previous eras, changes were required in speed, hand position, ball weight, and ball surface, but bowlers today must adapt in different ways to be competitive. Carry percentage has become a big factor in a bowler's ability to detect a workable breakpoint, which is the prime factor separating strikes from 9-counts. Therein lies the significance of reading lanes and knowing the proper equipment to use (see chapter 11 for more on equipment.)

In reading the lanes, right-handers must calculate adjustments for hitting the 1-3 pocket, and left-handers must calculate adjustments for hitting the 1-2 pocket. These pockets are 60 feet (18.3 meters) away from the bowler, who must deal with skid, roll, and hook at different angles on undetectable oil patterns. Golfers can recover from errant shots, and baseball pitchers have the luxury of eight teammates to bail them out of critical situations. But bowlers can pound the 1-3 pocket continually with no redeeming reward for their efforts. Stubborn 4-pins, 10-pins, 7-pins, and now, thanks to reactive balls, 9-pins have cropped up to further discourage bowlers.

As a rule, bowlers test all lanes by delivering the first ball down the 10th board in a straight line. The condition of the oil pattern will dictate the amount of hook. Follow the test illustrated in figure 2.2 to explore other areas on the lane. The more the ball hooks, the farther left you should move your feet. Move left or right according to the amount of hook you are experiencing. Begin by moving from the 2nd arrow to the 2nd or 3rd board, then back to the 3rd or 4th arrow, playing each angle from a different starting point on the approach.

If a ball is laid down on the 10th board, crosses the arrows at the 10th board, and ends up at the 10th board on the pin deck, it has zero hook power. If it ends up on the 17th board, it is in the pocket and has recorded a hook power of 7 boards.

If a ball is laid down on the 12th board and crosses the 10th board (second arrow), it will end up at the 4th board if it doesn't hook. Most professional players divide the length of the lane (60 feet, or 18.3 meters) into four separate divisions of 15 feet (4.6 meters). A nonhooking ball that is laid down on the 12th board and crosses the 10th board at the arrows will hit the 8th board halfway down the lane, hit the 6th board at 45 feet (13.7 meters), and cross the 4th board at the pin deck. However, an average hooking ball will reach a breakpoint at approximately 45 feet, break left toward the pins, and enter the pocket at the 17th board.

Hitting the pocket does not ensure strikes. The entry angle takes precedence over anything related to proper execution. Unfortunately, many young bowlers place great emphasis on delivering power balls with excessive revolutions. Although these deliveries create excitement with their destructive force, they are reminiscent of the old adage that "those who

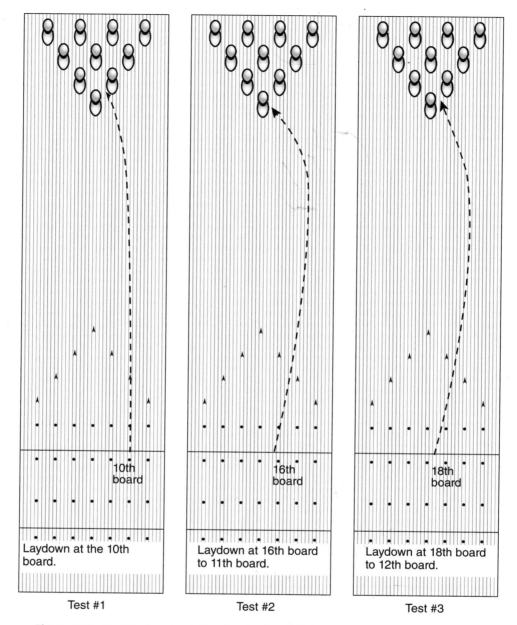

10th
board

16th
board

18th
board

Laydown at the 10th
board.

Laydown at 16th board
to 11th board.

Laydown at 18th board
to 12th board.

Test #1

Test #2

Test #3

Figure 2.2 Test the lane by delivering the first ball down the 10th board in a straight line. The more the ball hooks, the farther left you should move your feet. Move left or right according to the amount of hook you are experiencing. Begin by moving from the 2nd arrow to the 2nd or 3rd board, then back to the 3rd or 4th arrow, playing each angle from a different starting point on the approach.

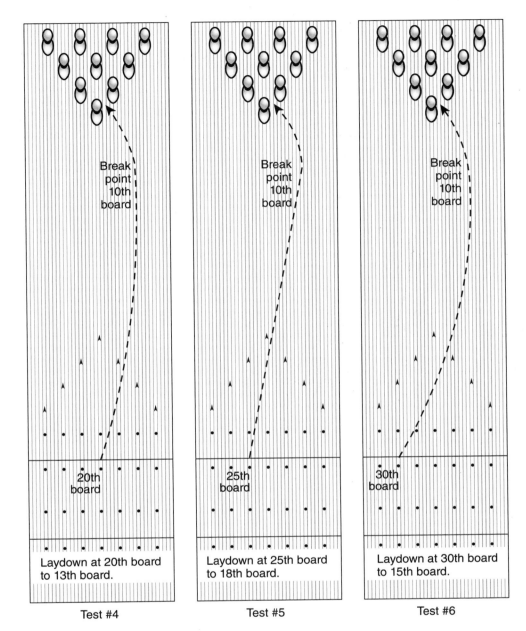

Break
point
10th
board

Break
point
10th
board

Break
point
10th
board

20th
board

25th
board

30th
board

Laydown at 20th board
to 13th board.

Laydown at 25th board
to 18th board.

Laydown at 30th board
to 15th board.

Test #4

Test #5

Test #6

Figure 2.2 *(continued).*

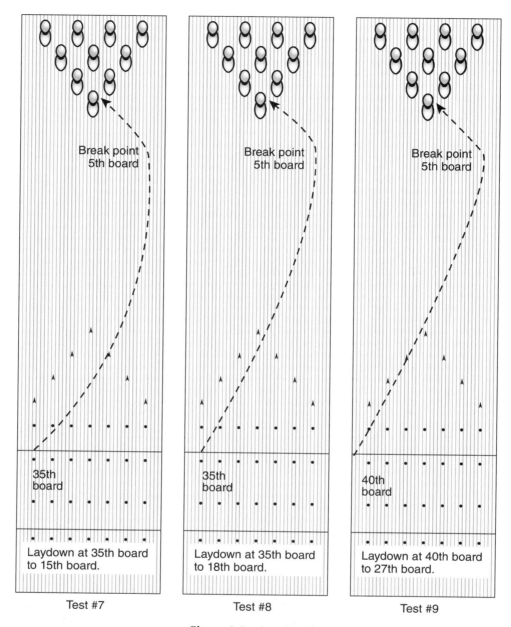

Break point
5th board

Break point
5th board

Break point
5th board

35th
board

35th
board

40th
board

Laydown at 35th board
to 15th board.

Laydown at 35th board
to 18th board.

Laydown at 40th board
to 27th board.

Test #7

Test #8

Test #9

Figure 2.2 *(continued).*

live by the sword die by the sword." True, bowling balls unleashed with brute power create bigger pockets, but they also tend to leave ungodly splits, such as the 2-8-10 and other wide-open splits resulting from odd entry angles.

Changing lane conditions necessitate strategic moves laterally on the approach. The moves contract or expand the arc of the ball to provide a more advantageous angle to the pocket. A one–one move means that the feet move one board laterally and one board at the crossing point, either right or left. Two–one, two–two, and other lateral moves are all devised to alter the ball's path to the pocket.

Dry heads (lanes that are dry on the front part of the playing surface) pose problems for players who throw wide hooks because of the high friction of the ball with the lane at the release point. Smart players move left to seek an oily area; others attempt to loft the ball over the heads. I have long objected to lofting the ball far out onto the lane. A lofted ball spins in midair and has a tendency to bounce when it contacts the lane. Consequently, it reacts irregularly on its path to the desired goal (see chapter 6 for more on releasing the ball).

Adjusting to lane conditions may necessitate moving strategically on the lane.

Dealing With Transition

Transition refers to any changes in lane conditions and has been an issue since maintenance crews began using oil on lanes. It includes carry-down, in which oil is relocated from the front end to the back end of the lane (carried by balls moving down the lane), and breakdown, which refers to the disintegration of the oil applied to the front of the lane. The recent advent of USBC (United States Bowling Congress) Sport Bowling has brought the issue of transition to the attention of bowlers everywhere, since Sport Bowling competitions always begin with a freshly cleaned and oiled surface (meaning it is free of carry-down).

The residue deposited in carry-down can help guide the ball to the pocket or affect how the ball rolls in the back end. The effect of carry-down on how the ball finishes may happen quickly or gradually, depending on the amount of oil originally applied to the lane and the amount of play on the lane. Breakdown affects the ball more dramatically; it can change the predictability of the ball as soon as the ball leaves your hand and hits the front part of the lane.

Bowling on a freshly oiled lane is like skiing on fresh snow, according to PBA champion Chris Barnes. Each skier who goes down the mountain carves ruts in the fresh snow. Skiers of the same style or level who leave from the same starting gate will likely take the same path down the slope, deepening the ruts and turning them icy and thus making the slope more difficult to manage. But amateur skiers who take different angles down the slope, carving unpredictable ruts into the snow, also create obstacles for a skier who just wants to get down the mountain in the shortest, fastest way possible.

The same scenario occurs in bowling. Oil is displaced on the lane in the same way that snow is displaced on the mountain. Bowlers with different styles and rev rates (rates of ball revolution) who play different angles will rapidly send a lane into transition. The smart bowler will recognize what is happening and decide on the best way to overcome it, both physically and mentally.

Many players today release balls at extremely high revolution rates. The combination of a 400-rpm release and an aggressive high-friction ball that flares across the lane will create rapid oil movement on the lane, as shown

Adapted from R. Shockley, 2002, "How to deal with transition," American Bowling Congress *Bowling Magazine* July 2002: 20. Used by permission of U.S. Bowling Congress.

by analysis using a Computer Aided Tracking System (C.A.T.S.). Such balls pick up fresh oil from the front of the lane (a process called *depletion*) with every high-speed revolution. This oil is then either removed from the lane completely or redeposited down the lane (carry-down). The more the ball flares, the more quickly the lane changes; the more bowlers who use this style, the more quickly the oil pattern is altered—all of which means lanes transition very quickly in today's bowling environment.

So what do you do? If the lanes don't react the same way in the late frames of your first game of the league season, you may correctly conclude that transition is the reason. You need to do something about it. Start with these tips.

First, observe how your ball reacts through the heads (the fronts of the lanes). You don't ever want to see any hook. If Chris Barnes notices any change, no matter how slight, in the front end (resulting in a 4-pin, usually), he quickly moves both feet and his target 2 boards to the left to try to find more head oil.

Second, observe ball reaction in the middle of the lane. Try to avoid heavy traffic—the proverbial ruts in the snow—by moving left. A player who uses a lower rev rate will often become stuck in this part of the lane if the lane is in transition. As the middle of the lane changes, the ball will usually come harder off the breakpoint, and the shot will go high on the head pin, leaving the 4-pin or splits.

Finally, pay careful attention to pinfall characteristics. Learn from the high hits. If you know the ball left your hand as intended and you hit your target with the right ball speed and rev rate, yet your ball still ended up on the nose or worse, then you will know that transition is at work on the lanes.

Overcoming a Tired Ball

If your ball looks tired around the 40-foot (12.2-meter) mark, you may think that the lanes are getting tighter or experiencing carry-down. In fact, however, your ball may be bleeding energy early, in the first 30 to 35 feet (9.1 to 10.7 meters), leaving nothing for the back end.

Overcome this problem by changing your ball and putting your hand more on the side of the ball to create 70 degrees of axis rotation (figure 2.3). This approach generates a stronger roll in the back end. The change in hand position slows the motion, allowing the ball to get to the breakpoint cleanly, since it won't read the middle of the lane as much, thus avoiding

Figure 2.3 Overcome a tired ball by creating 70 degrees of axis rotation.

early hook. Try changing to a weaker ball with a less aggressive cover, one with a strong-rolling core and dynamic drill pattern.

Going Inside

When he has to play the deep inside line because of transition on the lane, Chris Barnes adjusts his body setup and attack angle. When he is playing a more conventional up-the-lane angle, he squares his right side to the foul line and points his right foot up the boards (figure 2.4) to play right of the 10th board to the gutter.

When playing a deep shot, place the right foot in an open position, opening your entire right side to the lane (figure 2.5). Walk straight to the foul line, using the left foot for steps 2 and 4. Move the hand more to the side of the ball, creating a release with 70 degrees of axis rotation.

To gain velocity and projection through the hooking heads, stand taller and loosen your swing. Project the ball out on a flat swing past your calf; don't hit up on the ball. Lofting the ball is bad news for the lanes (bowling centers don't like it), and it creates erratic over/under ball reactions.

Figure 2.4 Go inside to play an up-the-lane angle.

Figure 2.5 Open the right foot to play a deep shot.

Adjusting Grip Pressure

Instead of making a ball change, Barnes will sometimes tackle the problem of transition by adjusting his grip pressure. He normally uses a relaxed fingertip grip with a 1/4-inch (0.64-centimeter) reverse in both fingers and a very tight thumbhole drilled forward at 1/16 of an inch (0.16 centimeter). He says this grip allows him to swing the force, not force the swing. He can make the ball hook earlier simply by tightening his grip on the ball. He can lengthen his swing by loosening his grip pressure, softly pushing the ball farther down the lane to the breakpoint.

Barnes is able to load his wrist on the downswing and unload it with great projection out into the lane (figure 2.6). His fingers stay well below the equator of the ball at the ankle and rotate up the back of the ball to well above the equator. This creates his standard 30 to 45 degrees of axis rotation and lots of revolutions.

Figure 2.6 To adjust grip pressure, *(a)* load the wrist on the downswing and *(b)* unload it with projection out into the lane.

In summary, use these tips to handle transition on the lanes:

✗ Be patient and stay calm. This is not a time to panic. Think about your options.

✗ Learn to manipulate your grip pressure.

✗ Try various hand positions and evaluate the effects of 20-, 45-, and 70-degree axis rotations.

✗ Learn to use your setup position to change the angle of attack and direct the ball well off your hand.

✗ Understand each ball's rolling dynamics and surface. About 75 percent of ball reaction depends on surface.

✗ Evaluate breakpoints down the lane. Learn to move the breakpoint toward you or toward the pins as needed depending on conditions.

✗ Use sandpaper and polish on the ball as necessary.

✗ Discover which pin positions work for your release style, rev rate, and ball velocity.

Remember, it isn't how much the ball hooks; it's *where* it hooks.

Overcoming the Reverse Block

Anyone who bowls on a heavily used lane will eventually come across the reverse block oil pattern. This pattern is usually not deliberate; it develops though use of the lane, as bowlers throw the ball in the middle of the lane to avoid the gutters. This usage dries out the middle of the lane but leaves oily areas near the gutters, creating a reverse block (figure 2.7). By contrast, the crown condition features heavy oil in the middle and dry areas near the sides.

The reverse block is by far the most difficult scoring condition for any bowler who throws a hook—and the greater the hook, the worse the scoring potential. Straight or back-up bowlers may be able to maintain close to normal averages, but even their scores will suffer as the lane continues to dry out. Since down-the-middle traffic never touches the outer parts of the lane, those boards, usually from the 2nd arrow outward, remain oily enough to cause balls thrown there to slide out, which often results in washouts or other splits and sometimes causes gutter balls. Any hook ball that touches the dry middle area will overhook wildly to the opposite side.

Although bowlers can use strategy to bowl better when facing this type of lane condition, overall scores are bound to be lower than with more favorable oil conditions. Since all bowlers on such lanes face the same problem, the most accurate bowler will usually wind up the winner, albeit with a score that is lower than usual.

Strategy A: Modified Inside Swing

A right-handed player using a modified inside swing will set his or her mark nearer the middle arrow (closer to the 20-board area) and move both feet farther to the left in order to throw the ball at a greater angle toward the gutter (figure 2.8). This method will provide room for the bigger hook to get to the pocket properly rather than going Brooklyn (i.e., hitting the pocket on the wrong side of the headpin). The danger is that too much release angle toward the gutter will let the ball go into the out-of-bounds oil near the edge and slide out without even coming close to hooking back toward the pocket. Use a lower-friction ball to allow for a less exaggerated inside line. Some bowlers use urethane balls for this shot.

Overcoming the Reverse Block text and illustrations adapted by permission of Rolf Gauger.

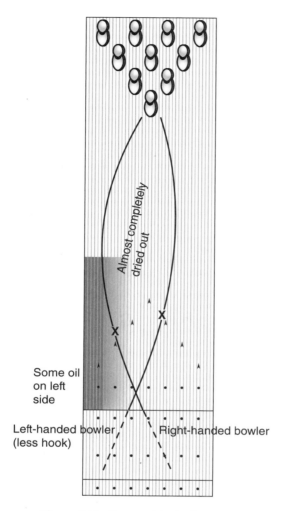

Figure 2.7 Reverse block oil pattern.

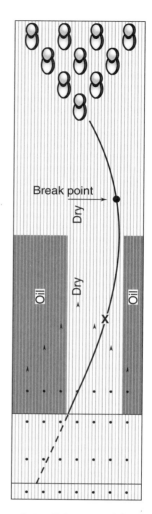

Figure 2.8 Using a modified inside swing to overcome a reverse block.

Strategy B: Inside Rocket to the Pocket

The inside rocket shot to the pocket (figure 2.9) is also a relatively far inside shot but with more ball speed. A slightly straighter hand release cuts down on the vicious hook, creating more potential for accuracy. This speed shot is recommended only for those who have mastered the technique. Trying to throw the ball harder—to muscle the ball—to increase speed can create huge accuracy problems.

Many bowlers who are unfamiliar with superdry conditions balk at the idea of an inside swing shot, but all better bowlers master it simply by practicing until it becomes more comfortable. This shot is worth practicing because the same basic shots are also used for overall dry lanes. It will definitely raise your scores. High-revving bowlers often have ball control problems on dry lanes unless they move deep inside.

Strategy C: Outside Down-and-In

The outside down-and-in shot (figure 2.10) can be a bit frightening for bowlers with lower averages. This shot requires a far-outside mark, usually around the 1st arrow or even out around the 3rd or 4th board. The feet are also outside. This approach keeps the ball in the oil portion at the edge of the lane for at least 30 feet (9.1 meters) before it starts to hook toward

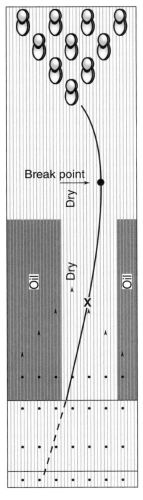

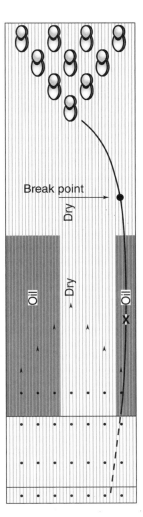

Figure 2.9 Using an inside rocket shot to the pocket to overcome a reverse block.

Figure 2.10 Using an outside down-and-in shot to overcome a reverse block.

the pocket. If the mark is missed on the inside, the ball will run away in the dry midlane area, so you should practice this shot before trying it in a game. A long-running, strong-finishing, reactive ball may work well for this down-and-in shot, because it will hook more effectively far down the lane. Again, this shot requires fearlessness and accuracy.

Left-handed bowlers will notice that their side of the lane normally dries out less than the right side does. Therefore, a normal shot area won't change as much. However, if the left-center part of the lane starts to overhook, a left-handed bowler should not try an inside shot—because of all the oil on the outside, the ball won't come back to the pocket. A left-handed bowler's best bet is to move his or her entire line farther outside, creating even more of a down-and-in shot than usual.

High-scoring, high-rev bowlers need to watch for the development of dry heads in this type of condition. Although broken-down conditions can often be mastered by lofting the ball, this technique won't work on dry heads. The ball will rev so fast before it touches the lane surface that it will jump about 1/16th of an inch (0.16 centimeter) sideways when it touches down, destroying accuracy and any hope of consistent scoring.

Lining-Up Checklist

Many bowlers use a checklist for lining up. Here are a few examples (reverse them for left-handers):

- ✘ Begin with a target line on the 10th board.
- ✘ On dry lanes, move your feet and target to the left.
- ✘ On slicker lanes, move your feet to the right.
- ✘ On dry heads, move left, find the oil, and play the oil line.
- ✘ When oil areas dry up, make one–one, two–one, and two–two adjustments (that is, one board left with the feet, one board left on the approach, and so on).
- ✘ When oil carries down, the ball will sometimes go through the breakpoint or break a bit late, leaving a weak 10-pin. You have two choices: Move your feet right to catch a breakpoint sooner, or start your approach about 2 inches (5 centimeters) farther back to compensate for the late entry to the pocket.
- ✘ When conditions favor a gutter shot (outside the 1st arrow), point the shoulder of your throwing arm inward about 1 to 2 inches (2 to

5 centimeters). This adjustment creates a feeling of an inside–outside swing and prevents pointing and pulling. It also eliminates gutter balls resulting from open shoulders that fail to close in time.

Remember that hitting the pocket with sufficient power is the primary goal for every bowler. But also remember that a strong mental approach, including reading and adapting to the lanes, will ease the task.

Gauging the Right Amount of Hook

How much hook is needed in order to be successful? Any hook with sufficient drive into the 5-pin is satisfactory. With proper angle and speed, an effective hook carries the 5-pin, which is the prime objective of a strike shot. (Grips, spans, and pitches play a major role in gauging hooking patterns; they are addressed in chapter 11.)

Hook is a means, not the end. A big hook is in no way a prerequisite for successful scoring. For example, Hank Marino, voted the top bowler in the first 50 years of the game by the Bowling Writers Association of America, threw a small hook with deadly accuracy. The diminutive Marino used a tight thumbhole in a two-finger grip. He often placed his thumb in the finger hole when the thumbhole loosened a bit. In choosing a tight-fitting thumbhole, Marino was in the minority; the majority of top professionals prefer thumbholes that are snug enough to prevent squeezing or dropping the ball yet loose enough to afford a quick release.

Joe Wilman, a great bowler from the Midwest, won the 1951 All-Star Championship (and twice finished second in this prestigious tournament), placed second in the 1951 Masters, and bowled his way into the American Bowling Congress (ABC) Hall of Fame with one of the shortest hooks in the game. Dick Hoover, the most accurate bowler in history, threw a slight hook, straight and hard. Hoover's record includes the 1951 All-Star Championship and back-to-back ABC Masters titles in 1956 and 1957. Although Hoover's excessive speed resulted in numerous 5-10 splits, he was no worse than an even bet to convert these splits into spares. ABC Hall of Famers Joe Norris and Joe Joseph, two of the smoothest and silkiest strokers of their era, delivered slight hooks with little effort and deadly accuracy.

Marion Ladewig, the unanimous choice among bowling experts as the greatest female bowler of all time, dominated the game as no one else, male or female, ever has. She was selected Bowler of the Year nine times, more than any other woman in the history of the game. Like her male counterparts, she delivered a straight ball, was exceptionally accurate, and rarely missed the pocket.

Understanding the Path to the Pocket

Bowlers looking to raise their games to a new level often discover that they have to learn a hook. Bowling is a target game, and the shortest distance between two points is a straight line. So why should a bowler forego the simplest, most accurate path—a straight ball—for a less predictable hook? The answer is action. To reach higher averages, a bowler must not only direct the ball to the pocket 60 feet (18.3 meters) away but also get it there with rotation and angle that maximize the potential for knocking down all 10 pins.

Whether the ball rolls straight or hooks, it has two basic motions: rotational and translational. *Rotational motion*, sometimes referred to as angular momentum, describes the act of an object revolving around its axis—for example, a wheel turning on its axle. The object may not be moving from one point to another, but it is still in motion.

A zero-degree axis of rotation is all forward roll. The rotation on the ball is in the direction of the forward travel, and the rotation will help keep the ball moving in the initial direction. The ball will roll out early and will not hook much. A bowler using this style will need to have his or her balls drilled to go long. In contrast, a 90-degree axis of rotation is all side roll; the rotation is perpendicular to the initial direction in which the ball is traveling. The ball hooks at a 90-degree angle to the initial direction because of the rotation. This style causes the ball to skid farther down the lane, then hook more. A bowler using this style most likely will need to have balls drilled to hook earlier.

One of the best discussions on ball movement during a well-executed delivery was written by Tom Kouros, a world-class coach and the author of *Par Bowling*. The information in this section is adapted from *Bowling Digest,* June 1995. Used by permission of Tom Kouros.

Translational motion refers to the motion required to move an object through space. When we say that an object has translational motion, we are saying that all of its parts are moving from one point to another with the same speed and in the same direction.

Using the numbers of a clock as a guide, with the headpin representing 12 o'clock, let's determine the general direction of a ball's translational motion as it comes into the lane. A bowling lane is approximately 18 times longer than it is wide. With the exception of some extreme angles of play, this geometric configuration means that the translational motion of most bowling balls, whether straight balls or hook balls, is directed toward the headpin (12 o'clock). When the translational motion of a bowling ball is directed at the headpin (12 o'clock), the ball will roll straight. If the rotational motion is directed to the left of the translational motion's direction, the ball has the potential to hook. If the rotational motion is directed to the right of the translational motion's direction, the ball has the potential to back up.

When the rotational and translational motions are moving in the same direction—say, 12 o'clock—there is no potential for the ball to either hook or back up. On the other hand, when the rotational motion of the ball is directed at 11 o'clock at the point of release, the shot has the potential to hook. Likewise, if the rotational motion of the ball is directed to 1 o'clock, the shot has the potential to back up. (We are referring to a ball rolled by a right-hander and are assuming the direction of the translational motion to be at 12 o'clock in all three cases.) Also, note the use of the word *potential*. A ball might have the potential to hook or back up, yet fail to do so because of excessive ball speed or a low coefficient of friction between the ball and the lane.

Furthermore, the greater the disparity between the direction of the translational motion and the direction of the rotational motion, the greater the potential for hook. For example, a ball with rotational motion directed at 10 o'clock at the point of release has the potential to hook more than a ball with rotational motion directed to 11 o'clock.

So, what makes a ball hook? To best illustrate the series of events that leads to a hook, let's imagine that a right-handed bowler has just set the ball down at the 10th board at the foul line and directed it toward the 10th board at the arrows. Thus the ball's translational motion is directed to 12 o'clock, while the rotational motion is directed to 10 o'clock. As the ball rolls down the lane, it will experience three stages of activity in its path to the target.

Skid

The first stage a ball enters is the skid phase. It will usually skid from the moment it makes contact with the lane through the first third of the lane, or roughly 20 to 30 feet (6 to 9 meters), depending on the amount of oil applied to the heads. The heads are the first 15 feet (4.6 meters) of the lane and are made of hard maple that can withstand continual pounding.

In the skid stage, the rotational characteristics of the ball have little to do with its course. To understand skid, imagine a smooth spherical object moving on a flat smooth surface, much like an automobile tire on ice. If the thrust is sufficiently strong, the object will skid instead of roll. In the case of an automobile tire, if the accelerator is strongly engaged, the tire will spin but not move. On the bowling lane, though movement is taking place, the ball and the lane are affecting each other only minimally. Consequently, the direction of the rotational motion (10 o'clock) remains unchanged throughout this stage.

Side Roll

During the second phase of the ball's course, it makes contact with the next 45 feet (13.7 meters) of the lane. This part of the lane is constructed of pine, which is softer than maple. The ball makes greater contact with the lane, and the motion of the ball continues toward its target sideways. This, in bowling jargon, is termed *side roll.* The ball continues on its course to roughly 3 to 5 feet (0.3 to 0.9 meter) from the pocket. At this point, the ball reaches its maximum forward trajectory, or *full roll,* and makes its leftward move into the pocket.

As the ball enters this second stage (side roll), the skid begins to give way to the effect of the ball's rotational motion and direction. In this stage, friction increases between the ball and the lane. The ball's rotational motion begins to exert influence on the ball, and the rotational characteristics of the ball begin to affect its path. Once friction between the ball and the lane reaches a critical level, the rotational direction (initially at 10 o'clock) begins to align itself with the translational direction (12 o'clock).

When the rotational direction of the ball begins to align itself with the translational direction, the ball begins to hook. The rotational motion is assuming some of the responsibility for translational direction. In other words, the ball's revolutions are now making stronger contact with the lane's surface, pulling the ball to the left to some degree and off its straightforward course, causing it to hook. The process wherein the ball's rotational direction aligns with its translational direction is called *precession.*

Furthermore, side roll is making its presence felt progressively, as is easily witnessed by the ball's hooking movement. At the same time, the ball track is steadily turning to the right toward a forward–roll direction (12 o'clock). As the old-timers would say, a ball is turning left to right when hooking right to left (or vice versa for left-handers).

To roll a hook, you must incorporate a release that allows you to effect turn so as to produce side roll (counterclockwise rotation for right-handers, clockwise for left-handers). In the simplest mode, side roll and its byproduct, hook, can be produced with a hand position that merely starts closed and remains that way (thumb position at 9 o'clock for right-handers). In fact, this technique is so simple that you might wonder why so many bowlers seek other ways of creating turn. The most popular reason veteran bowlers give for discarding this simple technique is its inability to produce a deeper and more pronounced side roll, which results in a more pronounced hook. Be aware that potential ball action isn't determined solely by the size of the hook. In truth, a player with moderate turn can outgun a horde of crankers, as was evidenced throughout the careers of PBA greats Earl Anthony and Don Carter. When it comes to turn, quality counts more than quantity. Ideally, a bowler should seek the type of turn that not only produces some hook but also is most effective in mixing and knocking down more pins.

Another misguided school of thought recommends using the wrist to create turn. Most bowlers who advocate this practice don't turn from the wrist as they think they do. Be leery of using the wrist as a primary source of turn, because that process inevitably leads to a number of topped shots.

When approaching the matter of turn, begin by determining what is required to make the ball's action formidable. First, you need hook, not only to produce a better angle of entry to the pocket, but also to enable you to tilt the ball for better pin action. Remember that without hook the axis cannot be tilted. Second, tilt the axis forward at the point of release so that the track of the ball is clearly positioned for maximum pin action at the point of contact with the pins.

To create both of these attributes, the ball must move to some degree off the inside of the hand, which requires the hand to be open to some degree at the point of release. Otherwise, the ball won't be able to move up and off the inside of the hand. Since the hand is partially open, a given amount of swing leverage is required to ensure that the ball will move up into the hand and off the inside, rather than coming off the front of the hand.

The best way to visualize this type of release is to picture a softball pitcher throwing an underhand curve. Arm speed is moderate through the downswing. The ball moves off the inside of the hand with a pronounced degree of counterclockwise turn. Making use of this technique when bowling not only produces ample turn and hook but also tilts the axis and positions it most favorably (forward) at the point of release.

Pocket Entry

For the third phase, let's examine the ball's reaction on entering the pocket. On a right-hander's ideal strike shot, the ball will come in contact with only four pins—the 1, 3, 5, and 9. All others are erased by the domino effect, better described in bowling terms as *pin deflection* or *pin action*. The 1-pin takes out the 2-pin, and the 2 deflects into the 4, which deflects into the 7; the 3-pin takes out the 6 and sends the 6 into the 10; and the 5-pin takes out the 8. This is generally regarded as the ideal strike shot.

Strikes have, however, been recorded in a variety of other ways. For example, a ball entering the pocket late (that is, slightly behind the head-pin) can result in a strike when the 6-pin is brushed by the 3-pin, then slides into the kickplates (side boards) and bounces back into the 10-pin. More often than not, the 6-pin will lie lazily in the channel and result in what is termed a *weak 10*. On other occasions, misguided shots have crossed over to the Brooklyn side (left-hander's pocket, the 1-2 pocket) yet produced a strike; these shots can be credited to luck. Additionally, a series of strikes can emerge from light hits that scatter pins into the left kickplates, then ricochet back into assorted pins still standing: the 5-pin; the 2, 4, and 5; or any other single pin or combination of pins that have remained on the deck. These fortunate strikes are referred to as *wall shots* and are also categorized as lucky.

Examining Different Ball Tracks

Before proceeding further, let's examine ball tracks—the rings formed around the ball resulting from the ball's contact with the lane and its subsequent entry into the pocket (see figure 3.1). There are seven types of ball tracks that indicate the spin applied to the ball and the impact it will have on the pins:

1. Straight ball
2. Back-up ball
3. Reverse hook

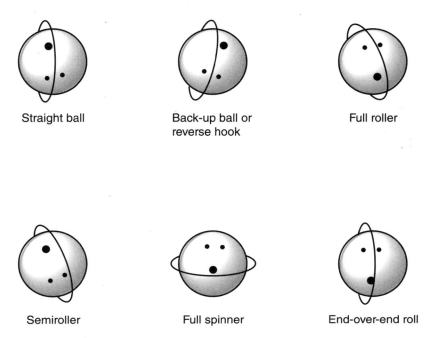

Straight ball

Back-up ball or reverse hook

Full roller

Semiroller

Full spinner

End-over-end roll

Figure 3.1 Different ball tracks.

4. Full roller

5. Semiroller (or semispinner)

6. Spinner

7. End-over-end roll

Different ball tracks result from different releases that produce disparate results.

Straight Ball

Throughout the history of the game, bowlers have been taught and conditioned to hook the ball, and understandably so. A ball that hooks into the pins produces a far greater percentage of strikes. This is by no means to demean a delivery directed in a straight line from a wider lay-down point at the foul line. Those who doubt the effectiveness of a straighter shot need only consider the success of some straight shooters who have bowled their way into the ABC, WIBC, PBA, and PWBA Halls of Fame. The game has been sprinkled with great bowlers who more than held their own by using straighter shots; relying on speed, angle, and precise timing; and covering less area in their path to the pocket.

The straight ball is released from an open hand, with no rotation of the fingers whatsoever. The straight shot rolls over the center of the ball, often over the finger holes or thumbhole. The track on the ball creates a noticeable rumbling sound when proficient players such as Walter Ray Williams and Norm Duke, two of the deadliest spare shooters in the game, throw at single pins. From the late 1940s through the early 1960s, Marty Cassio, a sharpshooter from Rahway, New Jersey, stood at the right side of the approach and used a straight shot to fire directly to the pocket (and eventually into the ABC Hall of Fame). Tony Sparando, another Easterner and ABC Hall of Fame member, used a straight shot and more than held his own with the best of his era.

Cassio and Sparando were, however, exceptions. The straight ball is basically ineffective as a strike shot. It has little or no power entering the pocket, and the deflection factor makes it a hazardous venture. Consequently, few professional bowlers employ this type of delivery for strike shots. Many elite players do, however, have the presence to use it for single-pin shots and those involving two or three closely bunched pins where no lateral movement of the ball is needed. In addition, straight balls are often thrown by older and beginning bowlers due to the simplicity of releasing the ball with minimal exertion.

Back-Up Ball

The back-up ball is the least desirable of all shots. Because it rotates in a path away from the pocket, it has no redeeming value as a strike shot. Although the track on this type of ball covers almost the entire circumference of the ball, the carrying percentage is substantially reduced by its deflective effect on contact with the pocket—particularly its inability to carry the 5-pin. Despite its deficiency as a strike ball, it does have positive uses for some players. For example, depending on lane conditions, Norm Duke sometimes throws a back-up ball at 10-pins. Mark Williams throws a back-up ball at the dreaded 2-8-10 and has on occasion converted this seemingly impossible split. But the back-up shot is hardly regarded as an offensive weapon.

Reverse Hook

A reverse hook is executed in the same manner as a back-up ball, with one major difference. Although both hand and finger motions rotate in a clockwise direction, the reverse hook is delivered with a stronger drive of the fingers from right to left, thus creating a pronounced hooking effect rather than the slower, fading roll of the back-up ball.

Except for Ernie Hoestery, no notable bowler ever notched a reputation delivering a reverse hook. Hoestery, a star player from the 1940s to the 1960s, sported a 200-plus average during an era when only the top players in the nation recorded 200 averages. The right-hander stood on the left side of the approach (a left-hander's stance) and released a reverse hook into the 1-2 pocket. Hoestery's ball had the same hooking effect as that of any left-hander, and, unlike the average back-up ball, it drove through the pins with little or no deflection.

Full Roller

The full roller is exactly what its name implies. The track on the full roller is formed between the thumb and finger holes, signifying an entry to the pocket with half of the ball on each side in the pocket.

During the 1940s and early 1950s, this type of roll was effective on shellac lane finishes. Many star bowlers delivered full rollers, including ABC Hall of Famers Ned Day, Dick Hoover, and Billy Golembiewski. During the late 1930s through the early 1940s, Ned Day was one of the most dominant players in the game. The highlight of his career was his victory over Paul Krumske for the 1944 All-Star Championship. Unlike Golembiewski and Hoover, Day was a true practitioner of the full roller. Billy G was a down-and-in player whose ball entered the pocket from a slight angle, and Hoover combined incredible speed and accuracy in his atom shot (right at 'em, that is) that went hard, straight, and right to the pocket. In contrast, Day delivered a slow, wide-arcing ball that crossed many boards and entered the pocket with tremendous force.

A full roller is thrown with the hand in a suitcase position at the starting point. *Suitcase position,* in bowling vernacular, means precisely what the term suggests: The fingers and thumb are lodged in the ball in the same way one carries a suitcase—on top. The hand remains in this position until the point of release. The thumb, at this point, is approximately at 10 o'clock. As the thumb exits, the fingers hit back and out in a clockwise motion with an open hand. Although a full roller tracks across half of the ball, it lacks the power produced by a side turn and enters the pocket more weakly.

When shellac lane finishes gave way to lacquer applications in the early 1960s, the change prompted better bowlers to alter their games by applying greater side turn to the ball. Unfortunately, this change diminished the careers of those who were unable to modify or adjust their releases. Although Billy G and Hoover continued to bowl well into the 1960s, Day was seriously hampered by the new lane conditioners and disappeared from the bowling scene. To my knowledge, no bowlers on the current PBA Tour throw full rollers.

Semiroller

This delivery is called the *semiroller* in some regions of the United States and the *semispinner* in others. (Similarly, oily lanes are referred to as *slow lanes* in some parts of the country, whereas people in other regions describe slick conditions as *fast tracks*.) At any rate, the semiroller, or semispinner, track is the most preferred delivery among elite players. The tracks on these balls are outside the thumbhole and finger holes and vary in many ways. Some tracks are closer to the fingers and a little away from the thumb; others can be just the opposite.

The semiroller track is closely related to the full roller. Whereas the hand and fingers in the full roller are positioned on top of the ball before the release and then rotate in a clockwise fashion, fingers in a semiroller are positioned at about 6 o'clock and rotate to 3 o'clock in a counterclockwise manner. Both tracks are very high and cover a greater circumference of the ball than is the case with the full roller. However, the semiroller track is just outside the fingers and thumb and is far more effective than that of a high roller because it combines the high-rolling effect with the side-turning movement to produce greater driving power into the pocket.

The semispinner is thrown with the hand well under the ball until the release point, at which time the thumb exits and all the weight of the ball is transferred to the fingers. At the release point, the fingers are positioned anywhere from 6 o'clock to 10 or 11 o'clock; they rotate in a counterclockwise manner, then drive the ball into the lane in an outward direction. (See figure 3.2.)

At the risk of confusing bowlers who have been trained to lift and turn, the term *lift* involves a misconception. Perhaps *propel* or *project* would better characterize the most suitable method for a proper release. *Lift* implies releasing the ball in an upward movement, but because the pins are on an even plane with the release area, it seems illogical to release in an upward course. The ball must be delivered *into* the lane, not up and *onto* the lane.

Proponents of the semiroller include smooth strokers such as Chris Barnes, Parker Bohn III, Brian Voss, and Pete Weber. Some semirollers

Figure 3.2 Danny Wiseman demonstrates a semiroller.

are thrown with minimum finger turn, thereby applying less hook and maintaining greater control. This was the system used by Don Carter and Earl Anthony, two of the most accurate players in history; they were uncanny at repeating high-quality shots in crucial situations and avoiding the creation of difficult spares.

Paul Colwell, a nine-time PBA titlist and winner of the 1974 ABC Masters, employed a release akin to tossing a flying disc. The hand is in a suitcase position until the release point: first, a quick exit of the thumb, then rotation of the fingers in a clockwise manner, up, then out and away. Despite the fact that Colwell's release resembled that of a full roller, his ball track was outside the thumb and fingers and was categorized as that of a semiroller. The list of great bowlers of the past who threw semirollers would stretch for miles.

Many older superstars delivered semispinners with excessive finger rotation. This group executed with less precision but, by virtue of creating a greater pocket, compensated by producing explosive strike shots that did not require the exactness of lesser-hooking balls. This method was the forte of older power players such as Don Johnson, Bill Lillard, Carmen Salvino, Harry Smith, and Andy Varipapa.

Spinner

A spinner tracks on the bottom third of the ball. With this type of ball, the wrist makes a spinning motion and the fingers end up on top of the ball at the release point. Naturally, the ball makes far less contact with the lane than one with a higher track does. Although this is the least-favored roll among elite bowlers, it served well for old-time stars Joe Norris and Joe Joseph.

The spinner shot contrasts sharply with the full roller, end-over-end ball, and semiroller, and it is far less effective on light hits and ineffective on oily surfaces. At the same time, bowlers who throw this type of ball relish dry conditions, where they enjoy an advantage over players who throw wide hooks and labor to keep the ball in play. Bowlers on the PBA Tour are often confronted with conditions that magnify hooking balls to such an extent that power bowlers (right-handed) are forced to deliver balls across the left channel to keep them in play. In fact, even the smoothest strokers are forced to move far to the left to lessen the hooking action on the ball and reduce the angle to the pocket. These conditions favor spinners and reduce others to mediocrity. Because this type of condition is not as prevalent on the PBA Tour's well-dressed lanes, bowlers who rely on spinners are normally disadvantaged, and this reality is reflected in year-end records, which favor hook-ball bowlers over spinners in every statistical category.

Axis tilt is a key component of the spinner. A full roller would show little or no axis tilt; the initial spin axis would be parallel, or nearly parallel, to the lane surface, and one rotation of the ball would cover the major diameter of the ball. On a spinner, the initial spin axis would be tilted up from the lane. The ball track would be far away from the thumb and finger holes, and one rotation of the ball would cover a much smaller diameter than for other bowlers. The spinner will get the ball farther down the lane before it hooks.

Several players on the PBA Tour throw spinners, and Tommy Baker has to be the leader of the pack (figure 3.3). He manages an explosive hook with one of the slowest deliveries on tour.

Figure 3.3   The spinner has worked well for Tommy Baker.

End-Over-End Roll

The end-over-end roll became especially effective with the appearance of reactive urethane balls that maintain a direct path to the pocket with little or no deflection. This delivery has greatly enhanced the games of several players who have mastered it, particularly Walter Ray Williams and Norm Duke. Bowlers execute this delivery by applying maximum forward roll with the hand fully under the ball. The ball is thrust into the lanes with virtually no side turn. The secret to this method of execution is minimum application of the ring-finger turn combined with accenting of the release off the middle finger in an outward thrust. An effective end-over-end shot resembles a full roller in its rotational movement, with one exception: A full roller is tracked between the fingers and thumb and has no side roll whatsoever. An end-over-end roll is tracked just outside the thumb and fingers, and although the track covers almost half of the surface of the ball, it rotates slightly leftward. However, unlike a semi-roller that evolves into a sharp hook, an end-over-end roll maintains an even arc and is far more controllable.

Although semirollers enter the pocket with greater force and require less accuracy, end-over-end rolls offer some advantages:

✗ They are far more effective in carrying high 4-pins.

✗ They are less likely to leave the 9-pin.

✗ They rarely leave such unsightly splits as the 2-8-10, the 2-4-6-8-10, and other leaves that result from sharp-hooking balls that snap suddenly on dry back ends.

Walter Ray Williams stands head and shoulders above all others who rely on end-over-end deliveries. And, strange at it may seem, very few PBA players exclusively deliver this type of ball. Conventional wisdom would suggest that others might be inspired to emulate the all-time money leader and holder of more than 40 titles, but as of yet none have attempted to follow in his footsteps.

Norm Duke, considered to be as good as Williams, comes closest to delivering an end-over-end ball in the way Walter Ray does. However, Duke, who is regarded as the most versatile player on the PBA Tour, uses an assortment of hand positions, speeds, and angles to achieve his purposes. Nevertheless, he has resorted to an end-over-end release with great success.

Chris Barnes, another versatile player, has established a reputation for his ability to conform to all lane conditions. Like Duke, Barnes can throw straight, hook it a mile, or deliver it in an end-over-end fashion, all with equal success.

Determining How Much to Hook

Although bowlers have been successful with all degrees of hooking action, one principle must be adhered to: Strikes cannot be achieved unless the ball carries the 5-pin. Wall shots have become prevalent, but competitive bowlers cannot rely on luck when championships and money are on the line. The 5-pin is the kingpin, the immovable object that challenges the irresistible force—the ball. Regardless of how hard or how soft the ball drives into the 5-pin, any contact greatly increases the possibility of a strike.

A weak 10- or 7-pin is a possibility on any given shot. However, single pins are hardly a challenge to accomplished bowlers, and although the dreaded 8-10 leave is possible, it has been virtually nonexistent during the reactive ball era. Strikes recorded by virtue of wall-shot, 5-pin blowouts are lacking in good execution. Any strike in which the ball does not carry the 5-pin results from luck. A 5-pin stand can result in a 5-7 split, a 5-10 split, a 2-4-5, a 2-4-5-8, or a 2-4-5-7-8—all difficult conversions. Single pins are duck soup compared to these dreaded leaves. Simply put, then, an effective ball has proper angle and speed, as well as enough power to carry the 5-pin, the prime objective of an ideal strike.

With slight modification, the old slogan "Let your fingers do the walking" can serve as sage advice to bowlers: "Let your fingers do the work." Players who hook the ball have a great advantage over those who are not quite adept at this art. And those who can deliver power-laden missiles by using specific finger positions to alter the trajectory of the ball have, in certain conditions, an even greater advantage.

Bowlers can be classified into the following groups: power players, strokers, spinners, and end-over-end shooters. These categories generally relate to the degree of rotation a bowler applies to the ball, and fingers play the major role in determining the ball's direction and amount of rotation. Power players deliver wide-hooking balls by combining tremendous thrust of the arm, wrist, fingers, and legs. Strokers, on the other hand, rely more on finesse and delicate touch.

Power Players

Power players deliver wide-hooking balls through substantial wrist, finger, and leg action. This type of bowler uses power derived from force. The art of hooking a ball begins with the starting position of the fingers and wrist. The middle and ring fingers can be placed anywhere from the 6 o'clock, 7 o'clock, or 10 o'clock position, with the wrist rotating counterclockwise for a right-handed player. The position of the fingers will determine the amount of hook; any of these positions can be effective, provided the thumb exits at the proper release point (that is, before the point in the forward swing where the hand begins to move outward).

To think about the amount of hook to use, let's begin with the technique offering the largest hook potential—one practiced by the PBA power players known as crankers. The wrist is slightly cocked, the thumb is as far outside as possible, and the fingers are anywhere from 8 to 11 o'clock. Positioning the fingers in this delivery can begin with the pushaway or open up at the top of the backswing. The hand position must remain open until the ball is a few inches from the release point, at which the thumb exits the ball. The thumb must never remain in the ball beyond the ankle.

All power bowlers play wide-sweeping hooks and actually widen the pocket, sacrificing pinpoint accuracy for power, but a power bowler's delivery is characterized by one of two distinct manners of execution. Most contemporary players perform with an extremely open hand, whereas some, particularly those of the old school, cup their hand.

Some power players, including Jason Couch, Amleto Monacelli, Robert Smith, and Pete Weber, open up their hand at the top of the backswing and apply an inside–outside rotation of the fingers to generate powerful revolutions (figure 3.4a). Others, such as Del Ballard Jr., Chris Barnes, Doug Kent, and Sean Rash, cup their wrist to deliver explosive missiles (figure 3.4b).

Players who cup their hands generally produce less speed than do the open-hand players. This is not to say that bowlers with more hooking action are more successful than players who use shorter hooks with greater accuracy. In fact, the winning percentage for the accurate shorter-hook

Figure 3.4 *(a)* Some power players, such as Pete Weber, prefer an open-hand position, *(b)* whereas others, including Chris Barnes, cup their wrist at the top of the backswing.

players far outstrips that of the power players, with two notable exceptions: Pete Weber and Amleto Monacelli. Weber has bowled with uncommon power and accuracy for more than 20 years, overcoming all barriers during an era that has moved from polyester to urethane to reactive urethane and then to proactive urethane. Despite some struggles with the high-tech equipment in the mid-1990s, he has demonstrated uncommon flexibility in mastering the modern game. Although Weber is categorized as a power player, he applies enormous torque to the ball with a smooth, undeterred, free-flowing armswing—which is the hallmark of a stroker. Weber embodies the true meaning of the phrase "putting fingers in the ball": All of his power is generated through finger rotation following a clean, crisp thumb release—free and easy. Weber is the epitome of the power stroker.

Monacelli, on the other hand, is the essence of the genuine power player. Like Weber, Monacelli possessed both power and accuracy. With the advent of reactive resin balls, Amleto, who delivered with a wicked snap of the wrist and an exaggerated follow-through, faced difficulty in attempting to harness his powerful delivery. He experienced inconsistent overreaction and fell into a minor slump. I had previously coached the affable Monacelli, and I arranged a practice session with him. I recommended a lower and less violent follow-through with greater extension. He practiced my theory and, in a short time, developed the proper combination. After this change, Monacelli returned to contention on the PBA Tour.

Dave D'Entremont may come the closest of any player to using the Pete Weber power stroke. Gigantic compared to Weber, D'Entremont generates as much power as anyone on tour, and he does it in a flowing manner, though he isn't as consistent as Weber. Rudy Kasimakis, also known as Rudy Revs, earned his nickname through his knack for applying incredible revolutions to the ball. Unlike most players, Kasimakis combines amazing torque with greater speed than the average bowler. He executes his delivery with minimal effort, despite the fact that it is generated from an extremely high backswing. Like Weber, Rudy exemplifies putting fingers in the ball. Some power bowlers are proficient and comfortable with wide-hooking deliveries. However, as with Monacelli, many of them have attempted to temper their shots to maintain greater control.

In summary, power bowlers generate greater revolutions on the ball than do other types of players. They cover more boards on the lane, sacrifice accuracy, widen the angle to the pocket, and rely on the ball's explosive contact with the pins.

Helping Robert Smith Attain Power *and* Accuracy

Robert Smith possesses the strongest strike ball on the PBA Tour. He not only throws a wide-arcing ball but also delivers it with greater speed than anyone else. Before Robert joined the PBA Tour, I coached him at San Diego State University, and he had stardom written all over him. Robert's release was awesome, but he negated its advantage with an extremely forceful follow-through that ended behind his ear. I advised him to temper his follow-through by extending his arm outward and minimizing the bend in his elbow. He heeded my advice, became a bigger star, and established a reputation in the amateur ranks that earned him a spot on Team USA for international competition.

After joining the PBA Tour, Robert experienced difficulty in controlling his wide-arcing ball. Since I had helped coach the youngster at San Diego State University, I suggested a modified Sarge Easter Grip to negate the violence of his strike shot. This drilling procedure involves a regular fingertip grip on the middle finger span and reduces the ring finger to a conventional span. I further recommended a forward pitch in the ring finger in order to considerably lessen the ring-finger rotation, which in turn reduces excessive side turn. With this approach, the ball maintains its power, but the violent snap as it enters the pocket is stabilized. Although Smith is far from an end-over-end player, his adjusted grip tempered the side roll and permitted him to perform with greater control. Not surprisingly, Smith's converted grip led him to five titles, including the 2000 U.S. Open championship.

Strokers

The number of boards covered by the ball does not dictate effectiveness. The smart bowler takes what the lanes dictate. A ball covering 4 or 5 boards is as effective as one covering 10 or 20 boards, because the name of the game is *angle*. A shorter hook into the pocket is far more effective than one entering from a severe angle; balls that enter the pocket late will hang corner pins and, in many cases, result in ugly 7-10 splits.

PBA statistics show that strokers display greater consistency than crankers do. Players who combine power with less effort (that is, power strokers) are generally among the leaders in all scoring categories. They are not, however, found in abundance. For example, PBA power strokers Chris Barnes, Parker Bohn III, and Danny Wiseman all combine power with delicate strokes and minimal effort, yet they cannot be categorized solely as strokers, crankers, or tweeners (that is, between crankers and strokers). Tweeners are pure strokers who lack overwhelming revolutions in their delivery yet apply sufficient drive in their strike ball to keep pace with the elite players on the PBA Tour.

A free armswing is the prime ingredient for strokers. It is the simplest and most relaxed method of execution. Nevertheless, a stroker is walking a thin line; that is, a stroker must maintain a firm wrist without sacrificing freedom of the arm. A stroker's hand position should be maintained throughout the delivery. The hand should be under the ball, the fingers should be placed somewhere between the 7 and 9 o'clock positions, and the thumb should be at about 2 o'clock. The fingers must rotate counterclockwise to about 3 o'clock; the thumb should never finish farther left than 12 o'clock on the follow-through. Finishing with the thumb past 12 o'clock will result in excessive spin and weaken the shot.

Because of the simplicity of their method of operation, strokers enjoy an advantage over power players and other types of bowlers. Strokers use less exertion, and they are always balanced, which minimizes errant deliveries. By covering less area on the lanes, strokers reduce the possibility of leaving difficult spares and splits caused by balls entering the pocket at extreme angles. Although good strokers do not generate as many revolutions on the ball as do power bowlers, they apply sufficient drive to the ball to produce strikes in a more accurate manner.

Chris Barnes heads the list of ultimate strokers, but the list must also include Parker Bohn III, Tommy Delutz Jr., Norm Duke, Steve Jaros, Doug Kent, Tony Reyes, Pete Weber, and Danny Wiseman. All of these players boast smooth and graceful approaches, clean releases, easy strokes, and soft follow-throughs. And they are always balanced. These strokers are perpetual cashers, consistent finalists, and perennial winners. They achieve their goals through finesse, and the physical problems that can be brought on by thousands of games on the PBA Tour—aches and pains and sore thumbs—seldom beset them.

Power players do enjoy one great advantage. When lane dressings are dry and oil patterns have been altered by excessive play, bowlers are compelled to extend the ball's path to the pocket. This condition forces bowlers to move farther left (for right-handers, or farther right for left-handers) to deter early hooking action. Bowlers must attempt to drive the path of the ball away from the normal target and seek a later breakpoint.

Developing a Rhythmic Approach

The approach in bowling is like a ballet movement: smooth, graceful, and naturally synchronized. It is the determining factor in maintaining a free armswing, proper balance, precise position for release, and a fluid follow-through. The approach is the catalyst for setting up high-quality shots with undue strain or exertion. When you become secure in your approach, your confidence enables you to bowl consistently—shot after shot, game after game.

The trademark of dozens of legendary bowlers is a rhythmic approach. Sheer power and dynamic strike balls are exciting, but the majority of top-rated players rely on perfect timing, finesse, and a free armswing to ensure success. The list of bowlers who mastered an ideal approach includes Earl Anthony, Tom Hennessey, George Pappas, and Dick Ritger. Current PBA stars such as Chris Barnes, Parker Bohn III, Tommy Delutz Jr., and Norm Duke have achieved tremendous success by blending exact timing with average finger rotation; in contrast, power bowlers use a more unnatural and vigorous finger rotation. Although rhythmic bowlers perform in an effortless manner, they personify textbook strokers who have taken advantage of modern bowling balls that explode on contact with the pins.

The approach consists of these elements:

✗ Number of steps
✗ Length and rhythm of each step
✗ Knee bend
✗ Power step
✗ Slide

Number of Steps

Most players excel by using four- and five-step approaches. Some use six or even seven steps. How many steps make for the best approach? Simply put, do whatever feels comfortable; the number of steps for an ideal approach is not etched in stone.

Three-Step Approach

Though not common, this approach was used by one of the greatest bowlers in history. Lee Jouglard, an ABC Hall of Fame member, took only three steps. He not only captured the first ABC Masters title in 1951 but also set an ABC singles record of 775, which stood for 29 years before it was toppled by Mike Eaton at Louisville in 1980.

The pushaway in a three-step approach is initiated with the first step off the left foot (right foot for left-handers) and is quicker than in other walking patterns. The three-step approach relies on a free swing because of the importance of the force created by the weight of the ball. This force is so important because a three-step approach does not provide as much momentum as one using four or five steps.

In fact, the three-step approach offers no benefit whatsoever to a high-quality game. Most of all, it is practically void of rhythm. A three-step approach places the ball into the pushaway before the feet move. More often than not, this abnormal method of ball placement produces an undesirable tilt in the pushaway and causes hastier footwork, which disrupts timing.

To my knowledge, no one on the PBA Tour employs the three-step approach anymore. Nonetheless, some older participants, as well as bowlers with relatively slight disabilities, smaller people, and youngsters in junior leagues sometimes use the three-step approach because they lack the ability to consistently coordinate a weighted object with a well-paced approach.

Four-Step Approach

Mike Aulby and Parker Bohn III have earned a place in the PBA Hall of Fame by using four-step approaches. Aulby (now retired) and Bohn have a lot in common. Both are left-handed, and both have surpassed the US$2 million mark in career earnings. Both have received the PBA's Steve Nagy Sportsmanship Award and are in the USBC Hall of Fame. Aulby is also in the ABC Hall of Fame, while Bohn is a virtual cinch when he becomes eligible. Both have ballet-like approaches that flow to the foul line in perfect rhythm. Both have won more than 30 titles, and both heeded my advice by reverting from a five-step to a four-step approach.

I had coaching sessions with Bohn during his early years on tour in the mid-1980s—sometimes into the wee hours of the morning. One of my first recommendations was a four-step approach. Since then, Bohn has become one of the most fluid players in the game. As soon as Mike Aulby converted to a four-step approach, he too established himself as one of the smoothest bowlers on the PBA Tour.

A four-step approach eliminates additional moves that can hinder a bowler's rhythm. I have strongly advocated a four-step approach to professionals and amateurs who were plagued by timing problems in five- and six-step approaches. Although some players I coached did not switch exclusively to a four-step approach, they rehearsed this method repeatedly to regain rhythm and timing. You can accomplish this by pushing away on the first step repetitively until the movement becomes natural.

The four-step approach is the standard by which all other approaches are measured. In other approaches, the pushaway *must* begin with the first of the last four steps. The majority of qualified coaches recommend a four-step approach for beginning bowlers, and understandably so. Because of its simplicity, it is the most prudent method for developing rhythm and timing. The principal requirement for a proper four-step approach is the simultaneous movement of the right arm and right leg on the first step in the pushaway (opposite for left-handers). This is the beginning of alternating movements of the arms and legs in rhythm.

A four-step approach works best with a free armswing, wherein the arms and legs react as pistons; each propels the other. That is, in a four-step delivery, if the pushaway coordinates with the first step, the movement and weight of the ball will develop the proper rhythm. To develop a smooth, rhythmic four-step approach, initiate a pushaway with a short first step (figure 4.1a). At this point, the ball should be suspended beyond the first step, a position that permits the ball to drop through gravity. Without hesitation, proceed into the second step (figure 4.1b). Continue your approach by letting the weight of the ball dictate the cadence and flow of the ensuing steps (figures 4.1c and d). It is extremely important to keep your footwork gentle and paced to conform with the swing.

Figure 4.1 Parker Bohn III demonstrates the ideal four-step approach: (a) The first step is shorter than the length of the outstretched arm; (b) the second step brings the back foot forward as the ball drops; and (c) the third step is short and quick, leading into (d) the fourth step.

Del Warren's Successful Transition to a Four-Step Approach

Del Warren, now retired from the PBA, was one of my pet projects. Warren began his PBA career using a five-step approach. A 6-foot-5-inch giant, he began his stance at the back end of the approach and took five huge, robotic steps completely devoid of rhythm. His backswing soared 2 feet (0.6 meter) above his head, and his bump-out armswing, which veered to the right in the backswing, left a lot to be desired.

Del sought my advice and became one of the most willing students I have ever had. I moved his starting position from the back of the approach to the first set of dots and converted him into a four-step bowler. Can you imagine his shock? He was forced to move his long body up about one-fourth of the distance on the approach and to change from five long steps to four short, delicate steps. Then he was expected to slide behind the foul line. Warren has long arms and legs, and this transition gave him a cramped feeling.

We began our practice session by lowering the ball position in his stance in order to lower his backswing. We practiced a softer pushaway whereby he was able to transfer the ball weight from the hand to the shoulder. I placed my fingers at his shoulder joint, set my palm slightly higher than his ball placement, and asked him to push the ball up to my palm gently. At this point, I told him to relax all his muscles and let gravity carry the ball into the backswing. We repeated this procedure without taking any steps until Warren could sense a loose, free armswing.

We initiated his approach by shortening his first step simultaneously with his pushaway, then had him proceed into the approach. With his arms and legs performing in piston-like fashion, Warren's approach became smooth, and he became one of the most improved players on the PBA Tour. His ball placement and pushaway, combined with a freed-up armswing and a rhythmic approach, converted him from a journeyman player into a legitimate contender. In addition to earning a spot among the top five finalists in the prestigious Firestone Tournament of Champions in 1986, Del captured two titles before retiring from the PBA Tour to accept a position with AMF.

Five-Step Approach

A five-step approach is identical to a four-step approach, with one important exception. To develop timing for a five-step approach, you must pause slightly after the first step (see figure 4.2). Do *not* apply any movement in the pushaway until the first step has been firmly planted on the approach. In this manner, you are positioned to trigger the pushaway precisely with the second step.

Figure 4.2 Pete Weber demonstrates the model five-step approach: *(a)* He pauses slightly after the first step, before *(b)* triggering the pushaway and downswing with the second step, then maintains a smooth rhythm in the *(c)* third, *(d)* fourth, and *(e)* fifth steps.

The slight pause prevents any movement of the ball before the second step. A premature movement in the pushaway produces an early swing and influences a release beyond the desired leverage point. This flaw can be as detrimental as a late swing, if not worse, since a bowler can compensate for a late swing by merely waiting for the ball to reach the release point; with an early swing, however, there is no room for adjustment. Some of the greatest players in the game—including ABC Hall of Famers Bill Lillard, Carmen Salvino, Harry Smith, and Pete Tountas—were successful at planting early and waiting for the ball. In contrast, early swings cannot be regulated in releases beyond the leverage point. This type of release is described in bowling jargon as *hitting up* on the ball, and it is an absolute no-no.

Earl Anthony epitomized the model five-step approach. He floated to the line and executed from a firm, balanced position. Unlike power players, Anthony relied on finesse, an automatic release, and deadly accuracy.

Tim Criss, Tommy Delutz, and Patrick Healey Jr., head a group of five-step *tweeners*, a term reserved for players who are categorized as neither power nor straight players. In essence, they are power strokers, which means they apply fewer revolutions on the ball than do power players. They are finesse players who forsake sheer power for balance and accuracy.

Walter Ray Williams also employs a five-step approach. Williams, whose precision and eye–hand coordination have earned him more than 30 PBA titles and half a dozen World Horseshoe Pitching Championships, is a rarity among PBA players. He is neither a power player nor a stroker. He is a straight player who uses an uncanny release that features an end-over-end roll and is delivered at various speeds with a thunderous follow-through. His five-step approach displays good rhythm and timing. Although his aggressive follow-through results in his rearing up at the line, he is able to maintain accuracy. He is rarely off target and is one of the deadliest spare shooters in the game.

Although most PBA bowlers prefer a five-step approach, some of the top stars have established reputations using six and seven steps. During the 1970s and 1980s, bowling fans marveled at the six- and seven-step approaches used by Mark Roth, who has been honored as one of the 20 greatest players of the 20th century. Like Lillard and several other older stars, Roth generated incredible power from a planted slide. Norm Duke, regarded by many of his fellow pros as the most versatile shotmaker on tour, takes five or six small steps, but, unlike Roth, Duke relies on hand position, speed control, accuracy, and finesse rather than raw power.

Despite the success of bowlers who use five or more steps in their approaches, I recommend a four-step approach. It enables you to simultaneously activate the pushaway and the first step much more effectively than you can by applying an extra step. If you're a right-hander, simply start the pushaway on the right foot (left foot for left-handers). Any movement before the pushaway step is excessive and requires precise timing; any premature movement or delay leading into the pushaway step will cause a lack of rhythm in the approach. After more than 50 years of close observation of many of the greatest players in the game, I have learned that bowlers using more than four steps encounter greater difficulty in shaking slumps than those who embrace the four-step approach. As in any other sport, a routine involving fewer and simpler motions provides the greatest chance for success.

Bowlers who use five-step approaches for additional speed can achieve the same result with a four-step approach by raising the starting position of the ball. This ploy elevates the backswing and automatically accelerates the forward swing.

Length and Rhythm of Each Step

The following guidelines apply to a right-handed player who uses a four-step approach (use opposite instructions if you're a left-hander):

• First step—In a four-step approach, the first step should be shorter than the length of the extended arm in the pushaway. Any step beyond the extension of the pushaway will impede the free fall of the ball in the downswing. Your body weight must be above your feet, but in order to use gravitational force the weight of the ball must be beyond the first step. Consequently, a short first step serves as the catalyst for a free armswing. Steps should be taken in heel-to-toe order; that is, the heel should make first contact with the approach, followed by the toe, in a natural walking step.

• Second step—The second step should be longer than the first. As the ball descends from the pushaway, pull and extend the left hand back and away, forming an airplane wing. This positioning acts as a counterbalance and keeps the shoulders and body in line with the intended direction of the delivery. At this juncture, the ball should be at the bottom of the pushaway, slightly past the knee, and primed for its path into the backswing.

Note that many contemporary players, particularly those who employ the power game, extend their nonbowling arms forward, thereby opening their shoulders for loading up their release. They usually drift leftward with open shoulders, then realign to the target before releasing the ball. (This technique is addressed in chapter 10.)

• Third step—Most instruction books suggest increased lengths (after the first step) throughout the approach. At the risk of agitating highly regarded instructors, many of whom are my friends, I am opposed to this philosophy. Although the third step is generally acknowledged as the power step, it is also referred to as the trigger step or the push-off step, and all of these terms allude to the main objective and importance of the third step. The terms *power, trigger,* and *push-off* all convey the central notion of initiating a driving force. To accomplish this important maneuver, you *must* make the step short and rapid. It is virtually impossible to push off on a step that is beyond the upper-body position. The primary purpose of the power step is to serve as the beginning of a forceful surge into the slide, which is described later in this chapter.

To achieve the desired surge going into the slide, then, use a short, rapid third step by simulating a sitting position. A short step allows you to assume a sitting posture that places your third step in a sturdy base for powering into the slide. This suggestion is not based only on theory. Short power steps are, and have been, the trademarks of *every* successful player, from older stars such as Earl Anthony, Don Carter, Don Johnson, and Dick Weber to modern players such as Norm Duke and Pete Weber. This assertion can be substantiated through PBA tape replays that are available to anyone inclined to dissent.

Knee Bend

The knee bend is an important component of the third step and a vital element of high-quality shotmaking, yet many fall prey to a great misconception regarding proper knee bend. I can't begin to tell you how many times I have heard someone say, "Bend your knee on your slide." This phrase seems like constructive advice, but it is far more difficult to perform than it is to convey. Doesn't it seem arduous to bend your knee from an erect position with a weighted object in your hand? How can anyone descend to this level abruptly and maintain any semblance of balance? Consequently, if you find it difficult to descend rapidly, you should begin your stance with a slight bend in your knees, gradually descend on the second step, and assume a sitting position on the third (power) step (figure 4.3). You *must* bend the knee. Tilting the body to achieve a low position is counterproductive and will result in rearing up on the release. A proper knee bend, in contrast, serves as the catalyst for the power step, and a well-administered power step can enhance your game in many ways. It prevents rearing up at the point of delivery and permits a low trajectory on the release. It is especially effective on oily lanes and permits the arm to extend outward instead of upward in the follow-through. In a well-executed delivery, the ball touches down on the lane like a plane on a runway and is seldom heard when it makes contact with the lane.

Figure 4.3 Danny Wiseman illustrates proper knee bend in the third step.

Walter Ray Williams uses a knee bend to execute a near-silent delivery. The only sound you detect in his release is the crash of the ball into the pins. In contrast, Ryan Shafer has achieved great success with little or no knee bend, but his good fortune can be attributed to his short stature. He naturally releases into the lane from a lower position, which minimizes bouncing of the ball.

Oily lane conditions create chaos for bowlers who deliver from a high position. A bounce on a well-dressed lane decreases the ball's solid contact with the lane surface and increases deflection in the ball on contact with the pins. On the other hand, releasing a ball from a *low* lay-down point on oily lanes decreases skid: The ball grips the lanes sooner and creates a stronger roll. So I recommend using a stance in which your knees are slightly bent. Descend gradually on the second step, then simulate a sitting position on the third step.

Power Step

The power step is a prominent movement in a model approach. Whether you call it a power step, a trigger step, or a push-off step—all suggestive of a launching point that affords maximum leverage—you must apply it in a refined manner. The concepts of smoothness and force are somewhat contradictory, but a delicate balance between the two is necessary for an ideal delivery.

The power step can be either the third step of a four-step approach or the fourth step of a five-step approach; just think of it as the step preceding the slide step. In either case, the power step must be short and quick (see figure 4.1c on page 56.) An even rhythm is important in footwork, but the power step is deliberately shortened to achieve a desired purpose: to create power in a delivery without throwing you off-balance. When you deliver a weighted ball from one side of your body to the other, you are prone to imbalance, which must be counteracted by other forces. Moreover, you must accomplish this counteraction with your body in motion. Although your arms and legs automatically function in an alternating manner, you must coordinate the steps precisely to create an ideal release point. Unlike the heel-to-toe steps in the first two steps of a four-step approach, the power step is initiated with a strong, deliberate push-off from the ball of the foot, which thrusts your body into the slide. This movement creates the force and thrust of the hand, thus permitting acceleration through the

The power step is deliberately shorter so the armswing can catch up to the body.

shot without muscling it through the forearm. The power step propels the body into a position to wait for the ball, thus allowing the weight of the ball to be balanced throughout the swing. This technique also prevents an early armswing that would force the ball beyond the sliding step. Remember the secrets to a great power step: Make it quick and short, then sit and push off.

Slide

A major manufacturer ran a shoe commercial on ESPN that featured David Ozio stressing the significance of bowling shoes in PBA competition. The commercial featured the attachment and removal of four Velcro inserts for soles and four for heels, producing 16 different combinations for sliding and braking. It was quite appropriate, particularly in view of Ozio's graceful approach. We've all grown to appreciate the fluid movements of such players as Ozio, Parker Bohn III, Dave Husted, and Brian Voss. All achieve powerful deliveries with minimal effort.

Bowling buffs in the 1950s through the 1970s were awed by the graceful approaches of performers such as Dave Davis, Tom Hennessey, Joe Joseph, and Dick Ritger, who displayed immaculate form at the foul line. Joe Joseph was perhaps the smoothest bowler in the history of the game. His delivery was so fluid and clean that his ball was silent when it made contact with the lane.

An ideal slide is initiated on the ball of the foot and terminated on the heel about 2 inches (5 centimeters) from the foul line, as shown in figure 4.4. A good slide results in proper balance and prevents straining of the body, but it isn't the only path to effective bowling, as is illustrated by the success of ABC Hall of Famers Bill Lillard, Harry Smith, and Pete Tountas. Lillard, possessor of the strongest ball of his era, *never* slid. He braked on his last step, waited for the ball to reach the release point, and then uncorked the most vicious strike ball I have ever seen. Lillard actually wet

Figure 4.4 Chris Barnes possesses a smooth, balanced slide.

his heel with a wet towel or with saliva. This tactic is known as burning rubber, since it leaves heel marks on the lanes. In Lillard's case, it made life difficult for bowlers who relied on smooth approaches, but it was not a ploy to psych out opponents—it was just Lillard's personal style.

Harry Smith, another super cranker, braked suddenly, hopped slightly to the right, and then ripped the cover off the ball. Smith's game was unconventional, but over the course of his career he led more qualifying rounds in PBA competition than any other player, including Ray Bluth, Don Carter, Dick Weber, and Billy Welu. Smith netted 10 PBA titles in his career and was probably denied several more because of the original PBA scoring format, in which all qualifying pins were dropped entering match-play competition.

Pete Tountas used a slow, methodical, five-step approach in a heel-to-toe motion. He actually planted his slide step. Pete waited for the ball and stroked a powerful strike ball, one that gave him an ABC Masters title.

Although the aforementioned players each made their mark in an unconventional manner, they are far outnumbered by players who slide fluidly and maintain perfect balance. To negotiate an ideal slide, you must remember this: The slide step does not call for the heel-to-toe method. A well-executed slide is initiated on the ball of the foot and braked on the heel.

Regardless of the number of steps taken, one basic rule must be followed. The slide step *must* conclude directly in line with the previous step—that is, in line with the third step in a four-step delivery or the fourth step in a five-step approach. Any slide that is to the left of the previous step for right-handed bowlers, or to the right of the previous step for left-handers, shifts the weight away from the center of the body and creates an imbalance. It places the release too far away from the ankle and results in a loss of leverage, and it can also result in a pulled shot. Therefore, the slide step must be in line with the preceding step. This counterbalance prevents the bowler from falling off the shot. It also keeps the armswing close to the body and prevents a flying elbow.

One of the major sliding mistakes made by amateurs and pros alike involves the position of the toe and heel in relation to the target. In an ideal slide, the toe and heel should be aligned directly with the target. Reactive bowling balls, however, have afforded contemporary power players the opportunity to drift leftward on the lane and realign to the targeted area, and a high-quality shot can be delivered in this style, provided that the toe of the sliding foot and the shoulder are aligned with the desired target area.

Herein lies the key to a high-quality shot. The toes *must* follow the line of the body. Although accomplished players such as Brian Himmler, Brian Kretzer, and Robert Smith have been successful in applying this technique, they sometimes become victimized in their realignment process, particularly when lane conditions are less than forgiving.

Don Carter, the dominant star of the 1960s, approached the foul line in near-flawless fashion, yet his style was very unconventional. He bowled from a low crouch, applied a muscled pushaway, pulled the ball into the backswing with a bent elbow, and shuffled to the foul line. However, he slid with his toes, heel, shoulder, and armswing *all* aligned to his intended target. He was the deadliest clutch bowler of his generation, principally because of his impeccable footwork.

Ray Bluth, an outstanding bowler, demonstrated the essence of proper balance. A right-handed bowler, Bluth slid with his heel at least 1 inch (2.5 centimeters) inward from his toe. His balanced position resembled a tripod in that all his body weight was evenly distributed over his sliding step.

John Forst is a member of the Kegel company's expert lane-maintenance crew. He is currently responsible for PBA lane conditions, as well as lane-maintenance procedures at major tournaments around the world. Before his association with Kegel, Forst competed on the PBA circuit for several years and exhibited an explosive strike ball; however, with the exception of a doubles title, Forst failed to capture a PBA championship. His failure to reach his potential was due principally to a faulty slide. John's hips were slightly wider than average and, in an effort to create a clearance in the forward swing, he inadvertently swung his body leftward, shifting

Straighten-Up-and-Slide-Right Drill

Superstars Chris Barnes and Parker Bohn III are two who employ the ideal approach that I refer to as "straighten up and slide right"—that is, with toes and shoulders pointed directly toward the target! If you are experiencing difficulty in sliding properly, you can correct the problem by rehearsing simulated slides without the ball, just as I suggested in correcting foot patterns. Take your stance, continue through the approach, then slide and force your heel and toes in the direction you choose. Repeat this drill until it becomes natural. Try to remember my choice advice: "Repetition creates habit."

Baseball players have two options for sliding—headfirst and feetfirst. Bowlers have just one choice: The body, the shoulders, and the slide must all be directed toward the target!

his heel 4 to 5 inches (10 to 13 centimeters) left of his toes. This, in turn, placed his shoulders and toes open 4 to 5 inches to the right of the target area, creating a side armswing that inhibited Forst's efforts at repeating high-quality shots.

Rick Steelsmith gained worldwide recognition as an amateur at the FIQ (Fédération Internationale des Quilleurs, the ruling body of international bowling) tournament in Helsinki, then proceeded to capture the 1987 ABC Masters title at Niagara Falls. He joined the PBA later that year and was a unanimous selection for Rookie of the Year. A shoulder injury took a tremendous toll on his career, but he returned after a 2-year layoff and established himself as a major force on the tour. Despite the fact that he was one of the best shotmakers on tour, a minor flaw in his slide inhibited his success. To a lesser degree than John Forst, Rick occasionally slid with his toes inside his heel (by 2 to 3 inches, or 5 to 7.5 centimeters), an error that results in a sidearm delivery. Although this flaw wasn't habitual, it sometimes hampered his ability to repeat high-quality shots, and Rick's 10-pin stands on seemingly good shots were proportionately higher than those of most PBA players.

Power Player's Approach

The textbook version of a four-step approach is this: Walk three steps in a straight line, then slide directly in line with the preceding step. This approach has become a rarity for many players in an era of explosive bowling balls. Today we see more and more bowlers drifting 10 to 20 boards leftward (for right-handers). These power players possess incredible hook balls that cover a path crossing 15 to 20 boards and enter the pocket at extreme angles; these bowlers rely on modern balls to increase their strike percentage.

Power players' system of execution is diametrically opposed to that of textbook bowlers. Power players push the ball to the left of their bodies, walk away from the swing, and open their shoulders in the last two steps. They slide anywhere from the 35th to the 40th board, lay the ball down somewhere between the 28th and 33rd board, cross between the 5th and 6th arrow, and send the ball to an area between the 5th and 10th board at the breakpoint. (All points depend on the condition of lane dressing.)

Brian Himmler, Brian Kretzer, and Robert Smith stand out among those who walk extremely leftward. When lanes permit them to open up, they open their shoulders and unleash explosive strike balls. Himmler's five-step approach features a unique, quick-skipping fourth step that triggers an extraordinarily high backswing and leads into an extended follow-through from the shoulder joint (depicted by Tommy Jones in figure 4.5).

Pete Weber, arguably the greatest talent in the game today, uses a five-step approach. He uses an extremely high backswing that he developed as a young bowler; small in stature, he was compelled to add height to his backswing to gain additional speed. He maintained this style and incorporated a smooth five-step approach with a clean, pure release. Weber drifts leftward and opens up the lanes, but, unlike other power players, Pete succeeds with unusually slow ball speed.

Power balls are exciting and impressive, and power players can be dominant on conditions that permit wide-hooking balls to carom off the

Figure 4.5 Power player Tommy Jones *(a)* opens the shoulders and *(b)* unleashes a powerful strike ball.

Perfecting the Approach

Mistake	Modification
1. First step is long.	**1.** Make certain you push the ball away beyond the first step. If the step is beyond the pushaway, it will prevent gravity from producing a free armswing.
2. Second step has excessive drift.	**2.** Reduce drift on second step. If the second step drifts too much, it necessitates opening up the shoulders to enable the arm movement to clear the hips into the backswing. This, in turn, requires you to realign your body to the intended target.
3. Third step is too long and too stiff.	**3.** Make the third step short and quick and try to assume a sitting position. If the third step is too long, it is almost impossible to bend the knee on that step. A good knee bend in the sliding step is contingent on a deep knee bend in the third step. The simplest method is to assume a sitting position and push off into the slide. This technique not only helps in overcoming the disadvantage of delivering a ball from a high position; it also thrusts the body forward and keeps the ball behind the leverage area, primed for acceleration at the release point.
4. Release position is too high on slide step.	**4.** Push off into the slide and make certain that the sliding foot is parallel to the prior step—preferably with the sliding toe in line with the target. A major key in sliding properly is to keep the toe aligned with the heel or slightly inside the heel position. A delivery executed with the toe not pointed in the direction of the target will result in a sidearm delivery and, most likely, a pulled shot.

breakpoints and drive into the pocket with incredible force. Opening up the lanes does not require pinpoint accuracy but rather affords power bowlers the luxury of playing an *area* rather than a certain board on the lanes. This is not, in any manner, meant as an indictment of power players. Many PBA players have managed to successfully harness their power under demanding conditions. Power bowlers such as Jason Couch, Amleto Monacelli, and Pete Weber have exhibited their all-around talents, winning championships in any and every lane condition.

Yet the bowling game is full of players—pro and amateur—who unleash dynamic strike balls yet have little to show for it. Timing and accuracy are far bigger advantages to bowlers than are high-powered missiles that lack the consistency for overall scoring. In many cases, a bowler's inability to compete at the highest level can be traced to a lack of proper footwork, timing, or release point.

Although many bowlers drift leftward intentionally, others have developed an unwitting tendency to move left. Several methods can be used to correct a drift. One is the age-old exercise of rehearsing a foot pattern on the lanes without a ball. Another is to place tape on the lanes in a desired line and repeatedly retrace the line with eyes glued to the tape. Repeat the procedure until it becomes routine.

Proper footwork is important in addressing spares, particularly for power players. While opening up the lanes on strike shots is a power player's forte, it is important in converting a spare to position the body and feet correctly. In trying to convert one-, two-, and three-pin spares, it is much better to focus on straighter shots, accuracy, and proper footwork than on drifting left, opening the shoulders, and delivering high-revolving balls. Always remember that accuracy and proper footwork simplify the game.

One–Three Key

Many players use certain keys to attain their goals. I refer to this exercise as the *one–three key* because it represents the most crucial area of concentration: the strike pocket. The focus here is on the four-step approach. Although many players employ five-step deliveries, all systems can be seen as variations of the four-step approach. The "one" of the one–three key— the first step of the approach—serves as the basic element of a smooth, fluid, and rhythmic approach and is a principal factor in a free armswing. The step must be short enough to permit the ball to fall by way of gravity during the pushaway (see figure 4.1*a* on page 56).

You can refine your technique by studying top professionals who have developed enviable armswings through perfecting their first steps and pushaways. Aspiring bowlers should study the pushaways of players such as Tommy Baker, Parker Bohn III, Tommy Delutz, and David Ozio. They all share one fundamental: great pushaway steps, regardless of the number of steps taken in the approach.

Five-step players should pause slightly after the first step to synchronize the pushaway with the second step (see figure 4.2a on page 58). This synchronicity has been the trademark of many great players from the St. Louis area, such as Ray Bluth, Nelson Burton Jr., Dick Weber, and Pete Weber.

The "three" of the one–three key refers to the third step of the four-step approach, commonly referred to as the power step. It is one of the most important elements of a powerful release. Think of the third step as the thrust of an airplane from an aircraft carrier, or perhaps the turn in golf. (The turn is the part of a golfer's swing in which acceleration at the explosion point requires the weight to be shifted from one leg to the other; this is where a golfer generates the power for driving the ball farther.)

The third step must be short enough to enable you to push off and power into the shot (see figure 4.1c on page 56). You can make this easier by taking a longer second step that will enable you to greatly reduce the length of the third step in rapid motion. The third step must be short enough to permit you to assume a sitting position, which you can facilitate by gradually bending during the second step. It is extremely difficult to apply knee bend in the sliding step if the preceding step is erect or less than fully bent.

The shortening of the third step can eliminate rearing up, a flaw that results in releasing the ball from a high position and, in turn, causes the ball to bounce rather than be fed into the lanes from a low post. The ball should enter the lane as if it were a plane landing on the runway or a flat rock skipping across the surface of a pond or river. An ideal release is one that does not produce a thud or bounce. Released correctly, the ball merely flows smoothly through the head part of the lane. A short third step permits a bowler to generate tremendous thrust going into the last step, whereas a long third step poses great difficulty for assuming a sitting position.

Study some of the pros. Notice that players with the most powerful deliveries take extremely short power steps. This was particularly evident in Marshall Holman's incredible release. Holman's power step was barely beyond the preceding step.

In addition, if you are to generate any leverage or power, your release point must be behind the toe. Your thumb must clear the ball by the time it is perpendicular to or slightly behind the shoulder joint, just before reaching the ankle area. The thrust generated by a properly executed third step, which propels the body forward, permits your hand to remain well behind your ankle joint before it accelerates and applies the necessary action for a powerful release. Power is the effectiveness of the delivery to carry out the 5-pin. You can succeed in this important aspect of the game by perfecting your approach, particularly in the first and third steps.

In summary, executing high-quality shots requires the combination of a relaxed swing, a rhythmic approach, a deep knee bend that enables a strong power step, and a smooth slide.

Relaxing the Armswing for Fluid Motion

Bowling instruction books recommend various methods for achieving a proper pushaway and armswing. Some suggest a shorter pushaway; others recommend a fully extended arm with the elbow locked. These diverse theories may present a dilemma for aspiring bowlers. This chapter addresses various styles of execution and identifies which technique typically provides the best results.

Pushaway

In my experience, a proper pushaway is one that produces a free armswing—that is, a muscle-free swing in which the movement of the arm is generated by the weight of the ball. You accomplish this by holding the ball in the right hand with the left hand supporting it (opposite if you're a lefty). The ball should be close to the body, about waist high (figure 5.1a). Initiate the pushaway with a small arc, forming a curl and going up and out as you enter the downswing (figure 5.1b). Do this arcing motion in a soft, smooth manner. The entire process is contingent on a muscle-free forearm propelling the arcing motion into a weighted swing from the shoulder joint. As the foundation of your bowling style, this form of execution greatly increases the quality and consistency of your shots.

Figure 5.1 Chris Barnes *(a)* holds the ball close to his body, then *(b)* initiates the pushaway with minimal force from the forearm.

Pushaway Variations

Bowlers use various styles of execution. Some PBA players (e.g., Norm Duke and Danny Wiseman) resort to shorter pushaways. A shorter pushaway is controlled; it is generally initiated from a lower position and directed downward rather than in an arc.

Other bowlers use full arm extension and higher backswings with great success. This group includes Jason Couch, Dave D'Entremont, and Amleto Monacelli. Although these men are all power bowlers and deliver extremely explosive strike balls, this does not mean that extended armswings add additional revolutions to a ball. The extended armswing just happens to be their preferred method of execution.

Walter Ray Williams, one of bowling's all-time greats, has garnered more than 40 titles using an end-over-end roll delivered via an extended arm. During the 1970s and 1980s, Swedish star Mats Karlsson notched four titles on the PBA Tour by using a fully extended pushaway with a locked elbow. Karlsson's strike ball was average at best, but he was one of the strongest spare shooters of his era. Mika Koivuniemi, an outstanding player from Finland, has also proven himself on American soil. He won the 2000 ABC Masters title and has been a consistent contender on the PBA Tour. Like Karlsson, Mika uses the fully extended pushaway with a locked elbow. Carmen Salvino was one of the great power bowlers from the 1950s into the 1970s. He began his career using an extended pushaway and threw one of the most potent strike balls of his era. In the latter days of his career, he began his stance with his arm fully suspended to his right side. He initiated his pushaway with the aid of his left hand, shoved the ball upward, and permitted the ball to descend on its own weight. Although this is not textbook technique, it encompasses all the elements of a free swing.

These examples demonstrate that professional bowlers have succeeded using various styles of execution. There is no set pattern, no absolutely correct system.

Correcting Common Errors

Pushaways can be altered to simplify execution, but those that are successful for some can be harmful to others. The early pushaway and the forced pushaway are the most common styles that can wreak havoc on bowlers' games.

Early Pushaway

Error: An early pushaway (that is, placing the ball into position before initiating the first step) results in an early swing, which commonly prohibits achieving a strong release point. (See chapter 6 for more on releasing the ball.)

Correction: The pushaway must coincide with the first step in a four-step approach (figure 5.2). This simultaneous movement is the principal factor in developing proper rhythm and timing and in producing a strong release. It prevents an early swing and allows you to wait for the descent of the ball in the forward swing, which can be accomplished only if the slide is firmly planted before the ball reaches the release point—an area at or slightly behind the ankle position. This is the strongest leverage point for an ideal release. In an early swing, the ball arrives slightly ahead of the slide, beyond the ankle and shoulder joints, which considerably weakens the shot. If you are faced with this problem, you can improve your game by initiating the first step a fraction of a second before beginning the pushaway.

Figure 5.2 To prevent an early swing, the pushaway must coincide with the first step in a four-step approach.

Although this strategy delays the swing, it will ensure that you achieve a greater leverage position.

In a five-step approach, there is one major adjustment. After the first step, *pause* slightly, then proceed. The pause prevents early movement in the pushaway and thus allows you to synchronize the pushaway with the second step.

Forced Pushaway

Error: A coerced or vigorous pushaway can seriously impair the free armswing and induce a tilt during the pushaway step. This, in turn, can impede the cadence and rhythm of the approach.

Perfecting the Pushaway

Mistake	Modification
1. Pushaway is muscled, vigorous, and too far out.	**1.** Relax the forearm. Place the burden of weight on the nonbowling hand.
2. Pushaway is shorter than the first step.	**2.** Place the ball softly beyond the first step to create greater weight in the swing.
3. Pushaway uses a downward projection.	**3.** Push the ball upward about 4 to 6 inches (10 to 15 centimeters) to engage gravity in the downswing all the way through the backswing.
4. The ball is pushed right or left of the body.	**4.** Relax all muscles, push the ball in the direction of the target, and let the ball fall into the backswing due to its own weight.
5. The ball is tilted on the pushaway.	**5.** Do not tilt until the ball begins to enter the backswing and forces a natural tilt.

Correction: Execute the pushaway in a soft, delicate manner, regardless of how you initiate it. Do not use a vigorous initial thrust in the pushaway; use a silky, easy pushaway with minimal force from the forearm. To influence gravity in the ball's descent, move the ball in an arcing manner before disengaging all muscles. Although I recommend my over-and-under theory (addressed later in this chapter and also in chapter 7), bowlers who subscribe to a suspended armswing à la Carmen Salvino can produce a good pushaway by practicing it from a lower position.

Armswing

Armswings can be classified according to three manners of execution: free, semicontrolled, and controlled.

Free Armswing

A high-quality pushaway is crucial in executing one of the most important parts of the game: a free armswing, also known as a pendulum swing (figure 5.3). Consider the pendulum on a clock. The pendulum swings to the right, then swings an equal distance to the left. Picture the top of the pendulum as your shoulder and the body of the pendulum as your arm: Your arm moves into the forward swing with force equal to that of the backward swing, *every time!* This action is a matter of physics. The centrifugal force, the weight of the ball, the height of the backswing, and the descent of the forward swing remain constant. Remember that relying on gravity is paramount to developing consistency. For example, if you use a 15-pound (6.8-kilogram) ball and gently raise it to a certain height, it will descend due to its own weight and go into the backswing to a certain height by virtue of gravity. The ball does not increase or decrease in weight; it follows the laws of physics. This is the ultimate key to consistency.

Consider this: Isn't it reasonable to assume that if you eliminate as many intangible factors as possible and build your game on a tangible factor, you will have a better game? That's called consistency. Countless times I've

Figure 5.3   Left-hander Parker Bohn III demonstrates the free armswing: *(a)* starting position, *(b)* pushaway, and *(c)* backswing.

Over-and-Under Drill

One of the most effective ways to develop a free armswing is to practice the over-and-under drill that I developed. This system has benefited many of my students—past and present. It not only helps bowlers develop a free armswing but also facilitates and improves a strong release point.

The drill is simple. It involves two imaginary bars, one at the starting point and one at the release point. Place one imaginary bar about 4 to 6 inches (10 to 15 centimeters) above the starting ball position. Push the ball *over* this bar, disengage all muscles in the forearm, and let the ball descend and swing due to its own weight. The *under* aspect of the drill involves releasing the ball under the other bar, which is located 12 inches (30 centimeters) above the foul line. The entire drill is contingent on one's ability to transfer the weight of the ball from the hand to the shoulder, which is the essence of a free armswing. I suggest taking a few preliminary swings before the pushaway to get a feel for the swing weight from the shoulder joint.

heard the lament, "My game lacks consistency." Adopting the free swing as the basis of your game will give you the consistency you've been looking for. You will achieve the same swing every time and develop a firm starting point from which to build and perfect your game.

Why do I consider a free armswing to be the cornerstone for ideal shotmaking? Check the records of any athlete. Other than those whose endeavors require brute strength, the most successful contestants are those who perform in a relaxed manner, devoid of muscle application. For example, in football, offensive and defensive linemen, linebackers, and fullbacks all rely on brawn and power. Conversely, those who rely on speed and deftness (the cornerbacks, wide receivers, and running backs) use a more mental approach: they employ agility to deceive and mislead their opponents. They achieve this craft through muscle-free athleticism. Quarterbacks Tom Brady and Peyton Manning sling precise passes that originate from muscle-free arms and lightning releases.

Basketball players are perhaps the greatest athletes in the world. Players who stand over 7 feet (2.1 meters) tall and specialize in dunking and blocking shots leave basketball fans in awe, but the most exciting players in the NBA are superstars like Vince Carter, Allen Iverson, Tony Parker, and Kobe Bryant, who demonstrate muscle-free agility to leave audiences breathless.

How the Free Armswing Helped David Ozio's Game

David Ozio, who joined the PBA in 1978, is a prime example of the benefits of a free armswing. Despite possessing one of the most graceful games in bowling, he had little to show for it monetarily in his first 6 years, winning a meager US$106,482 in 160 tournaments.

I met Ozio in 1985 at the Greater Los Angeles Open in Torrance, California. I was arranging a practice at a nearby establishment with David Husted and Kent Wagner, two Columbia staff members. Ozio, a studious bowler, was close by and overheard our conversation. When Wagner, Husted, and I arrived at the workout, Ozio was bowling at the opposite end of the lanes. Eventually, he came over and asked me to explain my free armswing theory. David Ozio possessed one of the smoothest approaches in the game. But despite his impeccable footwork, his release point was weak because of his semicontrolled armswing (addressed later in this chapter), which hampered his ability to execute high-quality shots on a consistent basis.

The over-and-under drill provided the foundation for my coaching session with Ozio. I began by placing my fingers on his arm at the shoulder joint. I placed my right palm about 20 to 24 inches (about 50 to 60 centimeters) in a direct line of his right shoulder. I instructed him to hit my palm with the pushaway, relax all the muscles in his forearm, and let the ball descend due to its own weight. We repeated this exercise several times, until he sensed the flowing sensation of the ball from his shoulder. After 30 minutes with Ozio, I returned to my other students. Within an hour, an excited Ozio came over and expressed disbelief at the improvement in accuracy and pin-carry. The following week, during the practice session at the Showboat Invitational in Las Vegas, we resumed our workouts. Ozio made the finals, finishing high in the standings. He then made the finals at the Quaker State Open in Dallas and continued to improve at the next two Florida tournaments. One week later, at the AMF Angle Open in Florissant, Missouri, Ozio won his first title. He won again later that year at the Tucson Open in Arizona. By the time the 1985 season was over, Ozio had earned more than US$85,000, which accounted for nearly half of his career earnings at that point. He now has 11 titles and more than US$1,300,000 in career earnings, was the Player of the Year in 1991, and was elected to the PBA Hall of Fame in 1995. Ozio is an advocate of the free armswing.

The top pitchers in baseball exemplify advantages of muscle-free execution. For example, pitchers Josh Beckett, Johan Santana, Justin Verlander, and Billy Wagner deliver fastballs at speeds of 95 miles per hour or faster, whistling rockets via unrestricted arms. Size may be advantageous, yet the small and wiry Billy Wagner routinely disheartens batters with 100-mile-per-hour (160 kilometer-per-hour) fastballs.

How do these athletes' techniques relate to bowling? Simply put, a free swing permits a player to release a ball more consistently at the power point than a muscled swing permits. Also, a free swing is far less exhausting and puts less strain on the shoulder than does a swing that is controlled and generated through the forearm. Superstars such as Mike Aulby, Parker Bohn III, Dave Husted, David Ozio, and Brian Voss have exemplified the advantage of a free armswing in bowling.

A true pendulum swing simply involves the movement of the arm generated by the weight of the ball. This is the basis for consistency. It is crucial to let the weight of the ball determine the peak of the backswing and the ensuing forward swing until the magic moment—the release point!

Although a muscle-free armswing is the prime objective, the placement of the ball in the pushaway does require a soft muscular application for completion of an effective shot. Place the ball into motion in a slight upward manner. At this point, disengage all muscles, transfer the weight to the shoulder joint, and let gravity govern the height of the backswing and the momentum of the forward swing.

A perfect model for a free swing would be to detach the arm at the shoulder, drill a hole in the arm, place ball bearings in the socket, grease it well, reattach the arm to the shoulder with a bolt, and then swing all motion from this area.

A free armswing was the trademark of Tom Hennessey, Joe Joseph, and Dick Ritger. These outstanding players gained ABC Hall of Fame status by virtue of free armswings, ideal timing and rhythm, and other essential traits for maximizing scoring potential without undue exertion. They were not known as power players, yet they held their own against opponents who exhibited thunderous strike balls.

The value of a free armswing in bowling can be understood in relation to the principles demanded in golf. Julius Boros, Gene Littler, and Sam Snead—three of golf's greatest players—exerted minimal physical effort and relied on muscle-free swings to achieve immortality. On the current PGA Tour, Ernie Els and Vijay Singh are poetry in motion: They demonstrate effortless, rhythmic, and, above all, muscle-free execution. If *you* can master the free armswing, it will signal the beginning of a better game.

Semicontrolled Armswing

I strongly favor the use of a free swing, but I think it is important to present other methods of execution because some bowlers are successful in exercising a more controlled swing. A semicontrolled armswing is executed with minimal muscle application. Numerous bowlers have accomplished outstanding results with semicontrolled armswings, and two of the greatest players in the history of the game, Don Carter and Earl Anthony, are renowned for their semicontrolled swings.

A semicontrolled swing is initiated with a downward or slightly upward motion and is controlled by a muscled forearm. Muscle is further applied to pull the ball into the backswing. At this point, all muscles are disengaged and the ball descends due to its own weight.

Don Carter, considered by many the greatest bowler ever, employed the epitome of a semicontrolled armswing. He began his approach from a low crouch, bent his elbow, drew the ball back with his forearm into a low backswing, and literally shoved the ball off his shoulder and down the lane. Earl Anthony, the most notable bowler of the modern era, was similar to Carter in several ways. Though Anthony stood more erect, he too applied a short backswing with a slightly bent elbow and, like Carter, pushed the ball down the lane. Unsurprisingly, Carter and Anthony rarely endured early hooking problems.

Marshall Holman, who was selected as one of the 20 greatest bowlers of the 20th century, addressed the pins with a slight bend in his stance. He lowered the ball with both hands at knee level. Holman initiated his approach by pushing the ball up slightly, then pulling it into a low backswing. Ordinarily, this technique would have resulted in a very early swing—an error that would place the release point *beyond* the leverage area. However, Holman took five short steps in rapid succession. His forward swing was free and smooth, and his quick feet *always* set him in position to wait for the ball before the release.

Pete Weber is the most successful contemporary player who often used a semicontrolled armswing (figure 5.4). To Pete's credit, his forward swing is one of the most fluid in the game, despite the fact that he executes it from an extremely high backswing. The unusual height of the swing can be traced to a pattern he developed in his early teens in order to generate speed. Pete's propensity for initiating his semicontrolled pushaway in a downward path has been a source of irritation in his career and occasionally results in an early swing that hampers his game.

Figure 5.4 Some players, such as Pete Weber, prefer a semicontrolled armswing.

I have had the pleasure of coaching Pete Weber on numerous occasions. I have worked with him on his downward pushaway and early tilt, which together produced a release point beyond his ankle. Our objective was to lengthen his swing to consume enough time to place the release point at or behind the ankle—the ideal release point. Our practice sessions focused on these two recommendations:

1. I suggested a slight upward motion to compensate for his downward pushaway. This was intended to lengthen his swing.

2. To address the early tilt, I suggested that he use a more erect approach and keep his shoulders back before he tilted into the backswing. The arcing movement of the ball, together with the elimination of the early tilt, delayed the swing enough to provide the proper release point.

Perfecting the Armswing

Mistake	Modification
1. Forearm muscles are flexed.	**1.** Relax the arm.
2. Backswing is muscle-pulled.	**2.** Use a soft upward pushaway to engage gravity for a free fall of the ball.
3. Swing bumps out (moves right of the hips in the backswing, for a right-handed bowler).	**3.** Realign bump-out swing by pushing the ball away slightly to the right.
4. Swing wraps around (moves to the left of the hips in the backswing, for a right-handed bowler).	**4.** Realign wraparound swing by pushing the ball away slightly to the left.
5. Downswing is forced.	**5.** Permit the ball to descend due to gravity's pull. Also try to keep the ball directly behind your elbow in the downswing until it reaches the flat plane of the forward swing.

Although Weber has been successful with a semicontrolled swing, I would not advise anyone to emulate his style. Pete cultivated this manner of bowling out of necessity, and his enormous talent in other aspects of the game more than compensated for his semicontrolled swing. As a matter of fact, Weber possesses one of the most fluid swings in the game. And, despite the fact that several other PBA stars have performed successful semicontrolled armswings, it is generally far more beneficial to use a free-flowing swing that is coordinated with the first step of a four-step approach or the second step of a five-step delivery.

Controlled Armswing

Few bowlers have achieved greatness with a fully controlled armswing. This style of armswing is controlled throughout—from the pushaway, to the downswing, to the backswing, and to the forward swing (figure 5.5). It is employed with full muscle control and appears robotic.

Figure 5.5 Although a free swing is recommended, Doug Kent has been successful using a fully controlled armswing.

Jim Godman, one of the PBA's top players during the 1970s, was one of the few successful players to bowl with a controlled armswing. He won 10 PBA titles, including the Firestone Tournament of Champions in 1973. He also carted off the ABC Masters crown in 1971. Godman was as strong as an ox and possessed forearms like those of a blacksmith. His technique was the epitome of the controlled armswing. Pete Couture enjoyed moderate success on the PBA Tour using the controlled armswing, and he currently ranks among the elite on the Senior Tour.

Mike Miller was another top player who used a muscled armswing. Miller established a wide reputation in bowling circles by exercising a thumbless delivery. He inserted his fingers into the ball and left the thumb supporting the weight of the ball; this technique made the controlled armswing a requirement for him. He resorted to this unusual method of execution as a matter of necessity. His inability to apply sufficient revolutions to his ball in a conventional manner compelled him to convert to a technique that would produce better results.

Miller joined the Tour in 1980, and in his first 10 years he bowled in 132 tournaments and won a total of US$92,691. At the beginning of the 1991 season, desperate and on the verge of retiring from the Tour, Mike decided to convert to a no-thumb delivery. The results were astounding. His strike ball became one of the most potent on tour and Miller experienced instant success. He captured the prestigious PBA National Championship in Toledo and finished the year with earnings of US$99,663, topping his total for the previous 10 years. He won two other titles—one at Wichita in 1992, another at Dallas in 1999.

Muscled armswings are not high on my list of recommendations. However, there is one point in favor of this type of delivery. With a bent-elbow backswing, the hand is lodged under the ball in a more effective position that permits the shot to get greater thrust from the back and inside of the hand, which in turn provides additional rotation and drive.

The greatest disadvantage of a muscled swing is the physical strain involved. Controlling a ball from the pushaway to the backswing and then through the forward swing requires inordinate strength and can injure the hand, arm, and shoulder. It is also far more difficult to generate speed without sacrificing accuracy. An armswing that is propelled by force cannot match the consistency of a muscle-free swing.

Bob Benoit and Bob Vespi, both now retired, exemplified the fully controlled armswing. Both players cupped the ball, bent their elbows slightly into short backswings, and forced the forward swing through a muscled forearm. A cupped delivery is similar to a thumbless delivery and places extreme pressure on the hand and forearm. If you do not have the arm strength of a Jim Godman, bowling in this fashion will inevitably take its toll and prove injurious. Not surprisingly, it disrupted Vespi's career and forced him to alter his method of execution. It also took a toll on Mike Miller in the early segment of the 2001 PBA Tour. The tremendous strain on Miller's knees forced him out of competition and necessitated surgery.

Bowlers have achieved stardom by using diverse styles and techniques: free armswings, semicontrolled armswings, and fully controlled armswings. The world is replete with athletes who attained stardom despite the fact that they performed in less-than-textbook fashion.

As I've said all along, and as I've seen in 60 years of observing the best bowlers in the world, a relaxed, free armswing is ideal for maximum effectiveness and continuity in your game. Are there instances when I recommend anything else? No. Although I recognize unconventional styles and the benefits that some bowlers gain from using other methods, experience has proven that the free armswing remains the standard of excellence.

Releasing the Ball

One of the most important aspects of sound bowling execution is a good release, which depends on placing the ball well back in the hand. At the release point, the thumb exits quickly, the weight of the ball is then transferred to the fingers, and the fingers project the ball into the lane. Some bowlers have moved toward a thumbless style because it allows them to put more revolutions on the ball, which can lead to higher scoring. But the thumbless style should be approached with caution due to its potential for causing arm problems.

Hand Positions

A leading American insurance company casts its representatives as the good hands people. Bowling certainly has its share of good hands people: those who have accomplished the art of changing hand position to achieve maximum hook, medium hook, or end-over-end roll; to straighten out a shot; or to throw a back-up ball. Proper hand position is the most significant factor in overcoming changes in lane conditions.

Many PBA bowlers rely on speed and spin to overcome diverse lane-maintenance patterns. However, while this philosophy may be successful for some bowlers, those who can change hand position enjoy a distinct advantage over those with more limited skills.

Not surprisingly, three of the greatest exponents of superior hand positioning—Norm Duke, David Ozio, and Mark Williams—honed their skills through grueling match-game competition in Texas. Duke's versatility can be credited to his innate ability to alter hand positions at any given opportunity. Chris Barnes' meteoric rise to stardom can also be attributed to his mastery of various hand positions, and Earl Anthony was masterful at changing both hand position and speed. Much like Anthony, Mike Aulby did not rely on an overpowering strike ball; he compensated by applying proper hand position, changing speeds, and maintaining accuracy.

Figure 6.1 illustrates the major paths to the 1-3 pocket for right-handers (1-2 for left-handers):

✘ Straight ball

✘ Back-up ball (reverse hook)

✘ End-over-end roll

✘ Wide hook

✘ Sharp hook

The following sections describe the hand positions necessary for creating these different shots. Instructions are presented for right-handed bowlers; left-handers need only reverse the directions.

Straight Ball

Beginners normally throw straight balls, and the smartest professionals utilize a straight shot for converting single pins, particularly 10-pin and 7-pin spares. It's agonizing to watch top-rated bowlers throw wide-arcing balls at single pins. This has been an Achilles heel for a number of PBA players, particularly when they are addressing single corner pins.

The proper finger location for delivering a straight ball is at the 6 o'clock position (see figure 6.2 on page 95). The wrist should be broken back, and the ball should be triggered by driving the two middle fingers straight through to the 12 o'clock position with no finger rotation whatsoever. Any finger direction other than straight through will radically affect the movement of the ball. A turn to the right will create a side roll that forces a leftward movement of the ball; finger rotation to the left will affect the ball in the opposite manner.

A straight ball can be delivered in two ways: (1) As the thumb exits the ball, the fingers do not rotate; (2) as the thumb exits the ball, the fingers do rotate, over the top of the ball, thus creating a spinning motion in its path to the pocket. The latter shot is referred to as a spinner and is susceptible to deflection on contact with the pins. Because of the deflection factor, this type of ball lacks the necessary drive into the pins and requires unerring accuracy for a high percentage of strikes.

Straight balls have become more useful for safety measures when counts of six or more pins are needed to ensure victory. The straight, hard shot

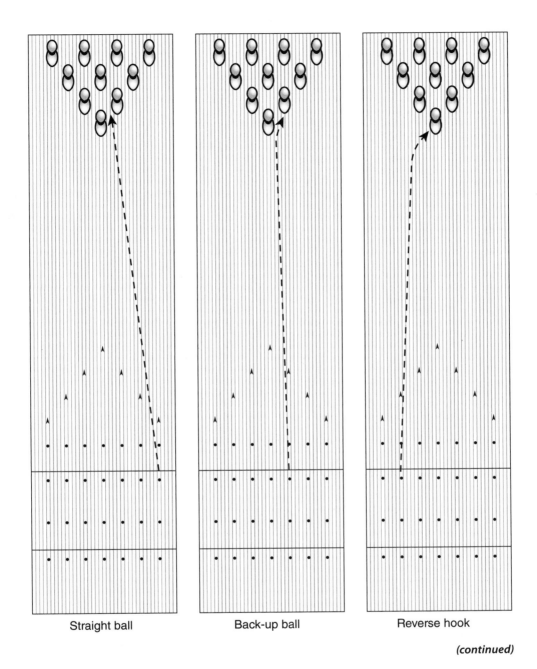

Straight ball   Back-up ball   Reverse hook

(continued)

Figure 6.1   The paths to the pocket.

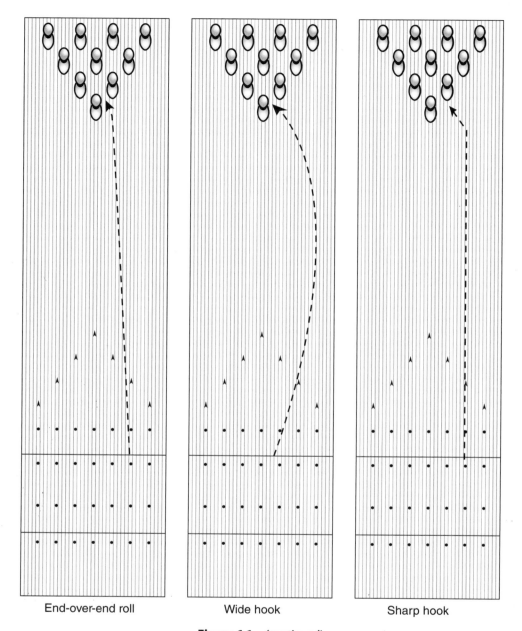

End-over-end roll   Wide hook   Sharp hook

Figure 6.1 *(continued).*

Figure 6.2   Hand position used to deliver a straight ball.

has become even more significant since Del Ballard Jr.'s ill-fated gutter shot on a fill ball that cost the burly Texan a championship against Pete Weber several years ago. Ballard needed seven pins in the 10th frame to clinch a win. Instead of playing it safe by throwing it down the middle hard and straight, he chose to play the extreme outside angle that had given him the comfortable lead. But the ball fell into the gutter. The horrendous result gave birth to the straight, hard delivery that PBA players now implement when counts of six or seven are necessary.

The PBA tour features several players who are considered straight players. However, bowling straight in the pro ranks does not mean throwing the ball completely straight; rather, it means assuming a stance farther right on the approach and directing the ball in a straighter path to the pocket. Players in this category include Roger Bowker, Michael Haugen Jr., Ernie Schlegel, and David Traber.

Back-Up Ball

A back-up ball, also known as a reverse hook, approaches the pocket in a manner opposite of the norm. Instead of hooking into the pocket, it moves away from the pocket, as if it were thrown by a left-handed bowler. The back-up ball is hardly regarded as a strike ball, except by beginners who lack proper instruction. Yet some of the PBA's top stars have effectively used this type of delivery. Norm Duke has mastered this shot for spare conversions of the 10-pin, and many players use a back-up ball when confronted with the dreaded 2-8-10 split. Mark Williams, one of the most proficient pros in the art of hand control, has had mild success in converting this extremely difficult split.

The back-up delivery begins with the fingers anywhere from the 3 o'clock to the 6 o'clock position. At the point of release, the hand rotates slightly clockwise (figure 6.3), rolling the ball from left to right. This type

Figure 6.3   Hand position used to deliver a back-up ball.

of delivery is recommended for proficient and experienced bowlers who apply this high-percentage shot at 10-pins or baby splits.

The reverse hook has become obsolete except in situations where a back-up ball is used to get the 10-pin. A few players practiced it more generally in the 1940s through the 1960s. Unlike bowlers who threw back-up balls at 10-pins or baby splits, they stood on the left side of the lane and used it as their strike shot. Reverse-hook bowlers applied extraordinary finger rotation from approximately a 5 o'clock position to an 11 or 12 o'clock position. The drive and path of the ball were very similar to those delivered by left-handed players, and, unlike back-up balls that deflect, reverse hooks maintained enough drive to carry through the pocket with efficient force. Ernie Hoestery, a standout player from New England, averaged between 200 and 210 in an era when only the most elite bowlers recorded 200 averages.

End-Over-End Roll

The end-over-end roll is the simplest shot for controlling the ball's path to the pocket. It has a great strike percentage and, though it lacks the thunderous impact of a hard-hooking ball, possesses enough rotation to carry out the 5-pin. The greatest disadvantage of this delivery is its tendency to leave occasional weak 10-pins, particularly when back-end lane conditions inhibit the added rotation required for maximum carry. This risk, however, is balanced by the shot's effectiveness in blowing out 4-pins and 7-pins. Furthermore, an end-over-end roll is less likely to leave a 9-pin. In this age of reactive and proactive bowling balls, 9-pins (8-pins for lefties) have become increasingly visible on strong pocket hits.

Walter Ray Williams has demonstrated an incredible ability to repeatedly place the ball in the pocket with an end-over-end roll. Williams possesses one of the highest strike percentages on the PBA Tour and rarely leaves more than two pins on any shot. Williams' Achilles heel is his occasional penchant to stray from his strong suit (the end-over-end roll) and attempt to compete with the big hookers. Overall, however, he is the most dominant player in the game—all because of his mastery of the end-over-end roll.

The end-over-end roll is one of the most effective deliveries for extreme outside lines with soft back ends. David Ozio has made a career of using the end-over-end delivery on gutter shots (that is, extreme outside angles).

For an end-over-end roll, the fingers are at the 6 o'clock position before the release (figure 6.4). The wrist is straight, and the ball is nested in the

Figure 6.4 Hand position used to deliver an end-over-end roll.

palm of the hand and rolled in a straightforward motion. The rotation of the ball must be generated from the *middle* finger to minimize side roll. The release must be completely free of any ring-finger turn; any application of the ring finger in the release will create undesired side roll. A modified version of the end-over-end ball is known as the curve ball, which requires a *slow* rotation of the middle finger from the 6 o'clock position to approximately a 4 or 5 o'clock position. The speed is slower, and the path of the ball is wider. This shot is more difficult to control but is advantageous on slicker surfaces, since its minimal spin and slower speed tend to create more friction on the lanes.

Wide Hook

I affectionately refer to the wide-sweeping hook as the *Hollywood shot* for its flash and exhilaration. Wide-sweeping hooks that cover 20 to 25 boards, or roughly 50 to 60 percent of the lane, create excitement and demonstrate raw power. Bowlers who use this type of delivery can generally be equated with baseball hitters who blast cowhides into outer space, even though their statistics may not be impressive at the end of the season.

Even so, all-time greats Bill Lillard, Junie McMahon, and Carmen Salvino (who later altered his game) bowled their way into Halls of Fame with wide-sweeping hooks. On the current scene, Dave D'Entremont, Brian Himmler, Robert Smith, and Pete Weber have done very well with wide-sweeping hooks. Although such players demonstrate tremendous hitting power, they also symbolize the old adage "Live by the sword, die by the sword." For example, former PBA players Scott Alexander, Kelly Coffman, Bob Spaulding, and Bob Vespi—great exponents of wide-arcing shots—have all departed the PBA Tour, principally because they were unable to control their delivery on spare shots.

The wide hook is undoubtedly the most potent, most vigorous of all deliveries for pin-carry potential. At the same time, it can result in the most bizarre spares imaginable, particularly on conditions played from outside angles. Grotesque splits like the 2-8-10, the 2-4-6-7-10, and occasionally the 1-2-3-4-5-7-8-10 splits have emerged since the advent of reactive urethane bowling balls.

The wide hook is executed in direct contrast to the end-over-end release. Finger rotation is paramount. In fact, fingers are positioned at 10 or 11 o'clock and rotate approximately two-thirds of a complete circle around the ball; the thumb never ends beyond the 12 o'clock position (figure 6.5). The thumb *must* clear the ball before it reaches the toe and the weight of the ball is transferred to the fingers. Before the release, the ring finger should be at about 11 o'clock, and all rotation must be generated by the fingers only. Again, the thumb position should never rotate beyond the 12 o'clock point; ideally, it should end up *at* 12 o'clock to prevent overspin.

The overwhelming advantage of wide-sweeping hook balls is the tremendous power generated in the delivery. Wide-hooking balls allow a greater pocket-entry angle and are far more explosive upon pin impact. This type of delivery also requires far less precision than lesser-hooking balls. In fact, the success of these shots depends on targeting not certain boards but a certain area of the lane.

On the other hand, the greatest drawback of wide-sweeping hooks is the difficulty in controlling ball movement. Although there are exceptions to the rule, most bowlers using this type of game are condition bowlers; that is, lane maintenance plays an important role in their performance. For example, the majority of proprietors around the country favor high scores. Lanes are dressed with considerable oil on the inside, and the last 15 feet (about 4.5 meters) of the lanes are bone dry. High-average

Figure 6.5 Hand position used to deliver a wide hook.

bowlers merely stand left on the approach, swing the ball out to the 6th or 7th board approximately 45 to 50 feet (13.5 to 15 meters) down the lane, and delight in the sweeping trajectory of the ball as it engages the surface with greater friction on the back ends of the lanes. By virtue of the oil buildup in the 1-3 area, the ball holds the pocket and produces a strike. This manner of lane maintenance has produced an unbelievable outbreak of 300 games and 800 series, and as of this writing nine instances of a 900 series have been recorded.

Most lane proprietors endorse high scores as a sensible business ploy. After all, bowlers who post high scores are more content and more inclined to return to a bowling center than they would be if they performed poorly. However, this type of lane maintenance has also created a rash of gratuitous 220- to 240-average bowlers while doing nothing to encourage a more skillful approach to the game. Moreover, these same players become demoralized in tournaments that require high-quality shots and skillful execution. Again, this is no indictment of skillful bowlers who have mastered the wide hook. Players such as Jason Couch (10 titles) and Pete Weber (24 titles) have mastered the game with wide-arcing shots, and multiple-time champions Dave D'Entremont, Ryan Shafer, and Robert Smith have also performed exceptionally well throwing wide-sweeping hooks.

Sharp Hook

A sharp hook is the safest and soundest delivery for effective scoring. It incorporates power and accuracy, and, although it does not have the tremendous hitting effect of a wide-sweeping hook, it is far easier to control and is less susceptible to missing difficult spare shots. The sharp hook was the trademark of such Hall of Famers as Ray Bluth, Buddy Bomar, and Don Carter. Other exponents of the sharp hook include Dave Husted, David Ozio, and Brian Voss—three of the steadiest and most accurate bowlers on the PBA Tour—who built very successful careers using this type of delivery.

Finger positioning for a sharp hook is similar to that for a wide hook, with one exception: Players who rely on wide hooks place their fingers farther under the ball, at approximately 10 or 11 o'clock, and rotate to 3 o'clock. Sharp hooks, in contrast, are performed with the fingers placed at 6 or 7 o'clock (figure 6.6a) and rotated to 3 o'clock (figure 6.6b). Bowlers who deliver sharp hooks cover far fewer boards and display greater accuracy, which generally makes them superior spare shooters.

Figure 6.6 In a sharp hook, the fingers start at (a) 6 or 7 o'clock and rotate to (b) 3 o'clock.

Release Point

A great release is the envy of every bowler not blessed with this talent. Even an ideal release, however, is ineffective—worthless, actually—if not executed at the proper release point.

What is the release point, and why is it important? An ideal release point affords an opportunity to launch the ball out on the lane from the strongest leverage area—one of the most important elements for consistent scoring. When done incorrectly, the release point is also one of the most difficult flaws for bowlers to detect. A faulty release point feels natural and leaves balance unaffected, yet the ball reaction is far from desirable. The ineffective ball reaction is usually the result of an early swing, wherein the release point is placed beyond the desired leverage area. Thus even a great release can be unproductive if not executed from a proper release point.

Here is a perfect analogy for determining an ideal release point: Envision a double-ball bag held in line with (or parallel to) the shoulder–ankle line. Lifting weight at this position places little or no stress on the arm and shoulder and allows easy maneuverability; thus it the strongest leverage area even as it allows proper balance. Similarly, if you place this same weight slightly behind the shoulder–ankle area, this position also affords easy projection onto the lane and allows proper balance. In contrast, if you set the identical load beyond the ankle–shoulder area, the weight of the ball forces the body forward, adversely affects leverage, and disrupts proper balance.

Preventing Early Swings

During the practice session of the 1999 PBA National Championship in Toledo, Tim Criss was experiencing difficulty in his ball reaction and sought my help. After a few minutes of observation, I detected his problem. Criss, a five-step bowler, was initiating his pushaway ahead of his second step, which resulted in an early swing that placed his release beyond the strongest leverage point. There are two strategies for achieving a proper release point and preventing early swings.

1. In a four-step delivery, initiate the first step a fraction ahead of the pushaway; in a five-step approach, begin the *second* step a tad ahead of the pushaway.
2. Speed up the approach.

Criss is renowned for an unusually slow cadence in his approach, so, rather than disrupting his rhythm, I recommended starting his second step slightly before his pushaway. This maneuver delayed his swing long enough to sufficiently place his release behind the ankle, with no appreciable effect on his slow cadence. Incidentally, Tim Criss won the tournament.

Preventing Late Swings

A late swing, on the other hand, indicates a late pushaway and possibly a rushed approach. A late swing inadvertently results in a forced forward swing (pull) if the armswing isn't loose. As with an early swing, a late swing can be altered by prompting the pushaway or slowing the approach. Because slowing the approach is detrimental to good rhythm and timing, I strongly suggest an earlier pushaway to overcome a late swing.

Again, the objective is to place the release point in the strongest position. Bowlers come in all sizes, so in order to reach a positive point of release you must take into account the length of your arms and legs. For example, a release point beyond the leverage area is a sign of an early swing, which can be attributed to one of two causes: a premature pushaway or a slow approach. Therefore, you must take measures to either delay the pushaway or speed up the footwork. You can solve the problem through the process of elimination: Try both methods until you determine which one allows you to reach the objective in the most comfortable manner.

Release

Hundreds of PBA players, as well as countless high-ranking amateurs, are blessed with great releases. Unfortunately, a great release does not ensure success. Many players display an aura of invincibility, unleashing high-revving missiles that rip the racks; in numerous cases, however, they suffer from faulty armswings, undue force, errant direction, or the inability to control the ball.

Contrary to popular belief, revolutions are not necessarily the key to great strike percentage. Shots with average revs, accurately delivered, are far more effective than wide-arcing shots that cover 15 to 20 boards and enter the pocket from extreme angles. These explosive missiles look awesome as they clear the decks with incredible force, but they are more likely to leave ringing 10-pins, solid 9-pins, hard 7-pins, occasional 4-pins, and the dreadful 7-10 split. Moreover, when back ends have been altered by oil carry-down, a wide-arcing ball often produces the ugliest of all splits, the 2-8-10. Although a ball with less rotation lacks the hitting power of high-revved missiles, its entry angle can equalize the strike percentage. Rather than execute a power release, this type of bowler—a stroker-type player—performs with a smooth stroke, accuracy, and proper balance. Although a great release is a coveted advantage, it does not ensure stardom.

What constitutes a great release? An ideal release is delivered with the hand well under the ball and the fingers starting anywhere from the 6 o'clock to the 7 o'clock position (figure 6.7). At the release point, a rapid exit of the thumb is a must. The weight is then shifted fully to the fingers, which rotate to the 3 o'clock position. Any rotation of the fingers beyond the 3 o'clock position, or of the thumb past 12 o'clock, will create spin instead of roll.

As stated previously, the major disparity between successful bowlers and less successful players is the release point—that is, the point of the

Figure 6.7   Chris Barnes demonstrates an ideal release.

Helping Marshall Holman Regain His Flawless Release

In 1986, Marshall Holman experienced his first major slump as a PBA player. Bowling at the PBA National in Toledo, Holman shot a most uncharacteristic score of approximately 250 pins under for the 16 games, placing him far down the list of qualifiers. For the first time in his career, Holman was discouraged, seemed lost, and sought my advice. After arranging a workout session at a nearby bowling center, I noticed two flaws in his game. The first was that his hand was out of place at the release point. Holman, whose release was the most envied on tour, was turning his hand too early and releasing off the side of the ball instead of remaining under it, thereby sacrificing all the potential power he normally possessed. Holman had a very short backswing, yet he managed a free forward swing. Therefore, I advised Holman to initiate his forward swing with his ring finger ahead of the rest of his hand. I urged him to maintain this hand position until the last split second before releasing the ball. After several minutes of continuous execution in this manner, Holman rediscovered his incredible release.

The second flaw was just as serious. Although he had reestablished his release, he was sliding away from the shot and losing leverage in the delivery. Holman's slide is much longer than any average player's. In fact, he was the only bowler I've seen on the PBA Tour whose slide continued after he released the ball. During our workout, I noticed his slide moving away from the swing line. This is an absolute no-no. The ideal slide must be in direct line with the preceding step to maintain proper balance and maximize leverage. Sliding away from the preceding step places the weight of the ball and body to one side and causes an imbalance. Sliding in under the preceding step forms a tripod. It keeps the ball in the body line and prevents a flying elbow—that is, a forward swing with the elbow outside the swing line and away from the strongest release point. Sliding in under the previous step also distributes the weight of the body evenly for proper balance.

After correcting these errors, Holman returned for his third qualifying round and shot 300 pins over for the eight-game block. Unfortunately, he was unable to survive the first cut. We continued the workout during the following week at Windsor Locks, Connecticut. Although Holman did not win that tournament either, he made the finals and headed for the crown jewel of the PBA tour, the Firestone Tournament of Champions. Armed with restoration of his talent and renewed self-assurance, Holman captured that title for the second time.

downswing that arrives at the flattest plane and affords the strongest leverage opportunity for launching the ball out into the lane. The rapid exit of the thumb is crucial because any ball delivered with the thumb in the ball beyond the sliding foot will result in hitting up on the shot (releasing the ball in an upward direction instead of out into the lane). Hitting up destroys the ball's effectiveness in several ways. A ball released in an upward manner is automatically spinning in midair before making contact with the lane, which can result in overreaction, an early hook, and a marked weakness in rotation.

Staying Under the Ball

Staying under the ball means keeping the ball well in the hand with the thumb on the lower side of the ball in cuplike fashion. Bowling manuals have suggested numerous methods for staying under the ball. Some have suggested closing the armpit from the top of the swing to the point of release. Jim Stefanich, one of the all-time greats, placed a towel under his armpit and kept it in this position throughout the swing. You could also try the Steve Hoskins method of keeping the thumb outside the ball from the top of the swing to the point of release. Or, you might prefer keeping the forearm facing the target from the release point to the follow-through, or perhaps keeping the elbow tucked into your side on the downswing.

These methods have been successful for many bowlers, but one fact remains: There are no set patterns. Bowling manuals merely serve as guides for attaining a desired purpose. I do not disapprove of any of the methods just mentioned, yet each puts undue strain on the forearm that may conceivably initiate muscle tension and deter the flow of a free armswing.

Experimenting With Different Releases

Power players such as Steve Hoskins, Amleto Monacelli, Ryan Shafer, Robert Smith, and Pete Weber all begin with the fingers at approximately the 9 o'clock position. Power strokers such as Mike Aulby, Parker Bohn III, David Ozio, and Brian Voss initiate their release with fingers at the 6 o'clock position and seldom rotate beyond 3 o'clock.

Danny Wiseman, a pure stroker, is an exception to the rule. He begins with the same hand position used by power players, yet he strokes the ball gently. Strokers rarely produce excessive rotation of the ball. It is important to note that all these players execute with minimal effort and a soft, flowing follow-through. Again, a great release does not guarantee success. Many players on the regular PBA Tour possess this innate talent

Ring-Finger Lead Drill

I devised a method to stay under the ball yet maintain a free armswing. I refer to my system as a *ring-finger lead*. In this technique, all movement is initiated from the hand during the lowest and heaviest part of the swing, thus requiring no muscle tension.

After reaching the top of the backswing, lead the downswing with the ring finger preceding the middle finger until the ball reaches the release point. At this time, the ring finger should be at about a 9 or 10 o'clock position. Then the thumb exits the ball, and the weight of the ball is transferred to the fingers. The fingers then rotate from the bottom to the 3 o'clock position, simultaneously projecting the ball outward into the lane.

and have attained incredible success, but an equal number have failed to take advantage of this important element of the game. For example, few bowlers can boast of a greater release than those of Joe Ciccone, Brian LeClair, or the recently retired Kelly Coffman and Joe Firpo. As of this writing, however, there isn't a singles title among them.

Several other types of release have proven very effective. Most notable is the one used by Walter Ray Williams. Walter Ray defies all odds for proper execution. He releases with extra effort, rears up at the line, and seems off-balance. However, he has a rhythmic approach, a loose swing, and the most incredible eye–hand coordination of anyone on tour. These traits have earned him six World Horseshoe Pitching Championships.

Williams' forte is his ability to keep his hand directly behind the ball. He applies little or no finger rotation, rolls the ball in an end-over-end rotation, and almost always places the ball in the 1-3 pocket. His strike percentage has been enhanced by high-powered reactive urethane balls with sophisticated core configurations. His deadly accuracy, coupled with the proliferation of modern explosive equipment, has converted Williams' previously weak 10-pins into strikes.

Butch Soper relied principally on accuracy by using a straighter line to the pocket. He released the ball with greater spin than do bowlers with average hooks. He accomplished this by rotating his fingers over the top of the ball, taking advantage of the increased friction enabled by advancements made in reactive bowling balls.

Roger Bowker, Ernie Schlegel, and David Traber also use a straighter path to the pocket, but they apply less spin with more roll. They do not rotate their fingers beyond the 12 o'clock position.

Several players on the PBA Tour have experimented with different hand releases that moved them from mediocrity to stardom. Norm Duke is a prime example. Norm was merely a journeyman bowler for many years until he began to experiment with assorted hand positions, speeds, and angles. He finally mastered his craft and, since this transformation, has become a favorite to win every tournament he enters.

Perfecting the Release

Release point

Mistake	Modification
1. Thumb in ball at release point is beyond ankle, usually because of early swing or very slow feet.	1. Do not place the ball into pushaway before the first step in a four-step approach. 2. Step gingerly for rhythm. Slow feet tend to disrupt rhythm and timing and induce an early swing. If increasing the cadence of the steps is uncomfortable or doesn't conform to the armswing, it is advisable to start the first step a fraction before the pushaway.

Release

Mistake	Modification
1. Wrist is lax.	1. Keep wrist firm.
2. Ball is not nested in the hand.	2. Place ball well back in the hand, and cup wrist at the top of the backswing.
3. Downswing has an early turn.	3. Lead the downswing with the ring finger.
4. Thumb is in ball too long.	4. Release the thumb at the flat plane of the forward swing before the ball reaches the ankle area. Transfer weight of the ball to the fingers and simultaneously accelerate and rotate the fingers and project the ball out into the lane. Do not permit the thumb to rotate beyond the 12 o'clock position.

Cup-and-Collapse Release

Numerous players on the PBA Tour use a technique I call the cup-and-collapse release. Del Ballard Jr. heads the list of contemporary bowlers whose deliveries fit this category. Chris Barnes and Sean Rash also feature this type of delivery.

This delivery can be performed in two manners: using a free swing or using a controlled or semicontrolled swing. In a free swing, you place the ball into the pushaway and let it fall into the backswing due to gravity's pull on the ball's weight. At the top of the backswing, cup your wrist and maintain this hand position until the release point. Then, collapse your wrist and drive the ball into the lane. This type of release creates a heavy roll and presents great strike potential.

In a controlled cup-and-collapse release, the ball rests back in the palm of the hand at the beginning of the stance. It is drawn back with a bent elbow, which remains bent throughout the swing. At the release point, the wrist collapses, and the fingers drive the ball into the lane. Although this is the ultimate method for staying under the ball, it can take a toll on the hand, wrist, and elbow. It can also affect the knees and legs. A number of PBA players can trace injuries to the strenuous exertion of the controlled cup-and-collapse release. This method of execution, in great part, curtailed and possibly ended the career of former touring player Bob Vespi. It also sidelined Mike Miller, whose thumbless delivery placed severe strain on his wrist and knees.

Many players who have been blessed with a great release have failed to take advantage of this gift. Again, a great release is not the guarantee for successful bowling. Average releases delivered at ideal release points—along with accuracy and balance—are the principal ingredients for a top-quality bowling game.

Two-Handed Thumbless Bowling Style

Jason Belmonte, who uses the two-handed thumbless style, participated in both the Malaysian Open and the Kuwait Open in 2008. If you haven't had the opportunity to watch this new breed of power bowler, you will be amazed at how effortlessly they create power and a high rev rate with a clean release.

Adapted from J. Slowinski, 2007, "How to coach or bowl with the two-handed thumbless delivery," *Bowling This Month*, July 2007: 6. Used by permission of Joe Slowinski and *Bowling This Month*.

The two-handed thumbless technique has emerged as a powerful new style that has produced amazing success for the relatively few bowlers who use it on the lanes. To illustrate, two-handed bowlers Belmonte and Osku Palermaa have dominated international competition in recent years. Belmonte, from Australia, won the High Roller in February 2006 and defeated Chris Barnes on his way to victory in 2007's World Tenpin Masters. In 2006, Palermaa, from Finland, won the AMF World Cup after dominating from start to finish.

Youth bowlers are beginning to embrace this style. In December 2006, two-handed bowler Chaz Dennis rolled a perfect game at 10 years, 2 months, and 27 days of age to become the youngest ever to roll a perfecto. Both of former pro Guppy Troup's children use the two-handed thumbless delivery, and 2003 and 2005 Junior Team USA member Brian Valenta is also a two-handed bowler.

The Chuck Lande Story

Although Palermaa and Belmonte have caught the fancy of bowling fans all over the world, they are by no means originators or creators of two-handed thumbless bowling. My first encounter with this unique bowling style occurred in 1989. Chuck Lande, a youngster in Dallas, participated in the PBA summer tour; although he was not a big winner, he was very impressive, and his subsequent impact on the bowling world is even more impressive.

Lande begin bowling in a youth league at the age of 12. He bowled with one hand during his first season and averaged a dismal 120. In 1978, Lande's mother purchased a ball for Chuck. The sporting goods cashier drilled the ball, and, needless to say, it was a lousy fit. Chuck couldn't even hold the ball, and it was too heavy. Consequently, he inserted the two fingers but not the thumb. The next season, he averaged close to 175, and by age 15 he was averaging over 200.

In his early years of bowling, Chuck accomplished some amazing things:

✘ He rolled his first sanctioned 300 at age 17 while bowling in the junior leagues.

✘ At age 18, he rolled back-to-back 300 games en route to winning the prestigious *Dallas Morning News* Match Game Championships.

✘ He rolled perfect games in more than a dozen bowling centers in the Dallas metro area.

Lande joined the PBA in 1986 and bowled virtually all Southwest Region events from 1986 to 1991. He won five PBA regional titles from 1987 to 1991, had at least five runner-up finishes, cashed in over 85 percent of PBA regional tournaments he bowled in, and qualified for the National Resident Pro Championships from the Southwest Region point list three times. It is important to note that the Southwest Region was one of the PBA's toughest during that period, featuring players such as Del Ballard Jr., Gary Dickinson, Norm Duke, Henry Gonzales, David Ozio, Mark and Mike Scroggins, Chris Warren, Tony Westlake, and Mark Williams.

Lande competed on the PBA summer tour in 1989 and learned three things:

1. He was good enough to compete with PBA players.
2. The lifestyle was a total beating and not very exciting.
3. The opportunity to earn a good living was not there except for Hall of Fame–caliber players.

In the mid-1990s, Lande begin fixing up computers at home and selling them to bowlers and bowling proprietors. By 2000, Lande owned a business that handled computer repair, refurbishing, and marketing. The rapid growth and success of the company made him think about retiring.

At Bowl Expo in 2001, Lande spoke about the need for proprietors to embrace computers and technology in their centers. During his visit to the show, he was shocked to learn how few proprietors used computers, had Web sites, or kept a customer database. Yet they all mentioned that business was great. He left the trade show with the desire to sell his tech company and build a center of his own in his hometown just outside Dallas.

He sold the company in 2002 and hired Howard Ellman, a designer he had met at Bowl Expo, to develop a concept for a modern bowling center. The result is the Rowlett Bowl-A-Rama, a state-of-the-art facility that has attracted league and casual bowlers; its 26 lanes are played by more than 200 youth league bowlers and about 800 adult league bowlers. Bowl-a-Rama is also home to former Junior Team USA bowler Jaime Foster, a 21-year-old female two-hander, as well as 7-year-old prodigy Anthony Simonsen, who continuously shoots games of about 230 using the two-handed technique.

Lande currently bowls three games a week in a competitive league at his bowling center and averages between 225 and 230. He still bowls two-handed and, claiming that modern balls are too powerful, typically uses regular urethane or polyester equipment. He hopes to bowl in PBA senior events when he turns 50 in 2014.

Chuck Lande's success is emblematic of the American Dream. He is arguably the most financially successful ex-professional bowler ever. Many big-name bowlers have taken advantage of their reputations and, with financial backing, achieved great success. Lande's wealth, however, is a result of his ingenuity and foresight—not to mention that he amassed his fortune by the age of 35.

Setup in the Stance

In two-handed thumbless bowling, the setup is fundamentally important to consistency and success. Specifically, in the stance, the balance hand should support the majority of the ball's weight. This hand should be placed in the front of and underneath the ball, just above the ball-side hand's fingers and the finger holes. This position allows for best support of the ball while not interfering with the fingers at release (a key consideration since, in this kind of delivery. the non-ball-side hand remains with the ball until the point of release). This positioning also keeps the balance hand close to the ball-side hand's fingers for support.

Start with the ball near the center of the body, just outside of center toward the ball side. Since this ball location is closer to the bowler's center of gravity, it allows the bowler to begin in a very stable position, better supporting the entire weight of the bowling ball. Starting foot placement should be the same as that used in a normal five-step delivery, and the first step is also similar to that in a normal five-step approach. Simply take a shortened first step created by the slide foot being in front of the ball-side foot slightly, about 1 inch (2.5 centimeters) in front for consistency.

Pushaway (Step 2)

An analysis of world-class bowlers who use the two-handed thumbless technique revealed a slight rotation of the hand to a stronger position in the pushaway. In essence, the bowler begins close to the 6 o'clock start position, then rotates to a stronger placement.

Osku Palermaa rotates his fingers to a 7 and 8 o'clock finger position as he pushes the ball away. This strong hand position is maintained until the release point.

As you take the second step, move the ball out and down while supporting its weight with your balance hand. As you move, rotate your hand to a strong finger position (7 and 8 o'clock for right-handers; 4 and 5 o'clock for left-handers). Make an effort to maintain this finger position until the point of release.

Palermaa is noted for his balance-hand position; he uses this hand to support much of the weight of the bowling ball. This positioning is an important component of the pushaway.

Skip-Steps (Steps 3 and 4)

Bowlers who employ a two-handed thumbless delivery use skip-steps in steps 3 and 4. These two steps resemble a gallop—rapid and quick. They function both as a natural timing element and as a mechanism to build tremendous power into the two-handed thumbless style. In short, the last three steps create a unique skip-skip-slide cadence.

The two-handed bowler is much like a high jumper or long jumper who generates power in the short–long step sequence leading to the launch at the end of the run. For the two-handed bowler, the ball transitions to the height of the backswing between steps 3 and 4. It is held at the top until the end of the fourth step. Due to the quickness of the two skip-steps, the ball is delayed in the downswing-to-slide transition, thus generating tremendous power.

As the bowler lands the fourth step, the ball reaches maximum height in the backswing. Due to the skip-steps, the bowler is briefly off the ground. The balance arm is just above perpendicular with the lane.

In the backswing, the balance hand is a critical component in supporting the ball and enabling the bowler to obtain height. This is, in fact, one of the benefits of the two-handed delivery: Using the non-ball-side hand to support much of the ball's weight reduces fatigue over time when compared with a traditional style.

Slide and Finish

The two-handed thumbless delivery has many release benefits. First and foremost, since the non-ball-side (balance) hand supports the ball until the release point, the bowler consistently achieves a very clean release. As the bowler enters the very short slide, he or she has created a very long separation between entering the slide and the ball position. This long separation creates power at the release, allowing the bowler to generate speed and revolutions. In addition, since the balance hand remains with the ball until the release, the bowler generates additional speed and power with the balance hand. As the ball leaves the hand, the balance arm makes a quick procession for balance.

Initially, many considered two-handed thumbless bowling a fluke wherein a few individuals had developed a unique style. But the amazing successes enjoyed by these bowlers have convinced coaches and players to look more closely. A thorough analysis of this approach and delivery reveals many consistencies among individuals who independently developed this unique but effective style while living continents apart from each other. Indeed, there is a future for two-handed thumbless bowling. No need to worry about a clean release. It is built in.

Release and Axis Rotation

Axis rotation is the single most important element of the release. There are four key references for creating distinct axis-of-rotation release angles:

1. Lead with the pinky through the target.
2. Lead with the ring finger through the target.
3. Go to 1 o'clock at the end of the follow-through.
4. Go to 12 o'clock at the end of the follow-through.

These techniques correspond to approximately 0, 20, 45, and 90 degrees. The references control the amount of hand rotation in the release. When you add the pinky finger and index finger, a bowler can easily develop, with practice, eight or nine more distinct releases with more consistent ball motions. The pinky will drop the axis rotation approximately 5 degrees from the base, whereas spreading the index finger will increase the axis rotation approximately 10 to 15 degrees. Leading with the ring finger, a bowler can do 15 degrees (pinky spread, index closed, ring finger leading though the target), 20 degrees (pinky closed, index closed, ring leading), and 30 degrees (pinky in, index spread, ring leading). With the thumb to 1, a bowler can do 40 degrees (pinky out, index in), 45 degrees (both in), and 60 degrees (index out, pinky in).

This release system really works and is simple to learn and implement. Of course, the hand position in the release is critical. At a minimum, the hand has to be behind the ball. The system works because these references and finger placements allow the bowler to vary wrist motion, from less to more, in order to create more precise ball motion.

In this system, the clock positions are relative to the ball-side shoulder. Thus a 12 o'clock position is straight toward the trajectory on the lane, not parallel to the front of the boards.

Osku Palermaa and Jason Belmonte have rightfully caught the attention of the bowling world by using the two-handed thumbless bowling style. They have dominated international tournaments for the past few years and energized young bowlers all over the world, just as Mark Roth inspired youngsters in the 1970s and 1980s with a vigorous, energetic method of execution.

Three notable Americans who use the two-handed thumbless style are former Junior Team USA member Brian Valenta, a left-hander; current Team USA member Cassidy Schaub; and Jaime Foster, who was voted women's Rookie of the Year in 2006 by the National Collegiate Bowling Coaches Association while competing for Pikeville College in Kentucky. Jaime started bowling with one hand but had to learn to use two after a car accident left her with an injured shoulder.

Developing an Ideal Follow-Through

One of the most important elements of a high-quality shot is the follow-through. An ideal follow-through is the culmination of proper execution, which results in balance, accuracy, power, carry percentage, and most of all, consistency. A good follow-through is delivered with a fully extended arm and minimal arm bend.

In the modern bowling environment, the art of proper follow-through has deteriorated, due primarily to permissive lane maintenance conditions that allow bowlers to merely stand to the far left, swing the ball out toward the gutter, and rejoice as balls bounce off the dry boards and head left into the pocket. Perhaps this sounds a bit harsh and demeaning, but unfortunately it is a fact. The proof lies in the inability of league bowlers with high averages to succeed on conditions other than those that have been tailored to produce fictitious scores.

Complicating the issue, bowling ball manufacturers have created balls that feature sophisticated cores with strategic pin placements surrounded by supercharged urethane covers. Designed to increase friction on the lanes, these balls have altered the game by allowing the ball to hook in ways it never could before.

Additionally, a bowler who wishes to refine his follow-through would be hard-pressed to sort through the available information about how to do so. Most instructional books and bowling manuals recommend reaching for the ceiling, following through with your hand behind your ear, and lifting and lofting. Personally, I have never supported the lift-and-loft philosophy, not even during the era of old rubber balls and shellac surfaces. And now, after observing the greatest bowlers in the world for the past 50 years, I feel confident that these antiquated methods of execution are far more detrimental than beneficial in the modern bowling environment. This is not meant to demean instructional techniques recommended by qualified instructors, but to enforce personal beliefs that have proven successful during my coaching career.

Delivering the Ball Into the Lane

Prior to the era of polyester and urethane coverstock, I might have suggested tossing the ball 3 to 4 feet (0.9 to 1.2 meters) out onto the lane in a downward trajectory—in other words, delivering the ball into the lane, in a fashion similar to landing a plane, rather than lifting and lofting.

I feel secure in my conviction that releasing the ball in an upward trajectory is counterproductive. Throughout my coaching career, I have strongly recommended delivering the ball *into* the lane, rather than up and onto the lane. Conventional wisdom dictates that balls delivered in an upward manner spin in midair prior to making contact with the lane, which inevitably causes the ball to bounce, overreact, and veer off course. In PBA lingo, this type of delivery is referred to as *hitting up on the ball*. Releasing balls on the upswing can result in weak 10-pins, buckets (2-4-5 for right-handed bowlers, 3-5-6 for left-handers), not to mention abominable splits.

In contrast, a ball driven into the lane from a low position is akin to landing a plane—soft and smooth, with minimal bounce. A properly delivered ball with a low outward follow-through will react like a flat rock thrown across a lake; the ball will skim along unimpeded. In order to accomplish this type of release and follow-through, I created the over-and-under theory (also addressed in chapter 5).

The *over* phase involves the ideal pushaway. Imagine a bar positioned about waist-high. Push the ball over the bar in order to create a free arm-swing. In the *under* phase, imagine a bar about 12 inches (30 centimeters) above the foul line and release the ball under the bar.

Following the release of the ball under the bar, replace *lift* and *loft* with *low* and *long*. The low-and-long system eliminates hitting up (which, in essence, means releasing the ball on the upward path of the follow-through rather than in the flat plane of the delivery).

Eliminate hitting up by thinking low and long.

Follow-Through Styles of the Pros

Reactive balls have profoundly affected the modern bowling game. The change is particularly noticeable among younger bowlers who are obsessed with wide-arcing balls that rip the racks on light hits. Modern missiles have also fascinated players who heretofore struggled in their efforts to apply sufficient revolutions to produce a high carrying percentage. In their desire to deliver powerful strike shots, many average players forego their normal games, exaggerate the follow-through, and rely on reactive bowling balls with strategically placed weights to maximize their scoring potential.

Knowledgeable PBA players also take advantage of ball surfaces, pin placements within the ball, and weight block designs. However, the successful ones combine this knowledge with proper execution—a motion that culminates in an outward, smooth, extended follow-through with minimal arm bend. Veteran bowlers such as Mike Aulby, Dave Husted,

David Ozio, Brian Voss, and Pete Weber seldom apply excessive effort in following through on their shots. Each performs in his own style, but all conclude their delivery in a fluid manner, fully extended, with little or no force applied.

Marshall Holman, one of the greatest players in PBA history, was generally regarded as a power bowler. Yet even though he possessed one of the most potent strike balls of his era, the Medford Meteor also used one of the most fluid strokes in the game. His follow-through, generated from a short backswing, was extended in an outward direction. He truly was a power stroker, and the PBA has featured numerous power strokers who bowled their way into the Hall of Fame, among them Dave Davis, George Pappas, Dick Ritger, Jim Stefanich, and Billy Welu.

An aggressive upward follow-through is far less effective than one stroked in an outward direction. Revolutions on a ball do not result from extraordinary force applied through the forearm but are generated through the fingers. Observe the deliveries of Chris Barnes and Robert Smith, two of the PBA's brightest stars. Both players possess unusually potent strike balls, and both follow through with arms barely bent and always outward.

In contrast, Pete Weber's follow-through is extremely high, yet very effective. This is due simply to the fact that Pete's arm is fully extended and unbent, and the follow-through is executed from his shoulder instead of his forearm. Weber's high follow-through is principally a result of a high backswing that he developed as a youngster. Small in stature, Pete cultivated this style to generate speed and, through the years, mastered it. Although I would not recommend Pete's method of bowling, he is certain to land in every Hall of Fame possible.

Walter Ray Williams stands out among players who use a hard-driving follow-through. Williams employs this style not to produce more revolutions but to generate more speed. Speed is a necessity in Walter Ray's game because he relies on an end-over-end roll. He is far less effective when he attempts to abandon his specialty shot and match players who excel on hooking conditions. However, his uncanny eye–hand coordination keeps him fairly competitive on dry hooking conditions. Nevertheless, his greatest advantage lies in an end-over-end roll, which is extremely effective with reactive bowling balls but tends to roll out if not delivered with sufficient speed. That is why Walter Ray uses a vigorous follow-through.

As stated in other chapters, there are no set standards for success. Although a smooth, fluid follow-through is recommended, there are exceptions to the rule. For example, only a fool would deny the tremendous success achieved by Mark Roth. Mark revolutionized the game in the early

Chris Barnes' delivery and follow-through. He demonstrates how to follow through with the arms barely bent and always outward.

Pete Weber uses a high follow-through.

1980s by uncorking one of the most thunderous strike balls in bowling history. He placed his fingers in the most extreme manner for maximal turn, at about 10 or 11 o'clock. He then released the ball with tremendous counterclockwise finger rotation to the 12 o'clock position. Roth is credited with inspiring thousands of youngsters to use this type of game.

A number of today's young power players use a fiercely accelerated follow-through. Diminutive PBA star Ryan Shafer of Elmira, New York, unleashes one of the most potent strike balls on tour and maintains one of the highest averages among professionals. Unlike softer strokers who follow through in an outward direction, Shafer rips through the ball with excessive force in a skyward direction.

Kelly Coffman, who retired from the PBA Tour a few years ago, used a muscle-driven follow-through. Coffman delivered the strongest ball on tour, producing as many as 24 revolutions. His power was generated through incredible upward motion with the forearm. Despite the crushing effect of his strike ball, Coffman was often victimized by inordinate spares and wide-open splits—common pitfalls for wide-arcing balls that enter the pocket at extreme angles. This is by no means intended to slight numerous power players who exert enormous energy in following through. PBA stars Jason Couch, Dave D'Entremont, and Brian Himmler all apply firm acceleration in finishing off their shots.

Parker Bohn III, one of the premier left-handers on the PBA Tour, has one of the most fluid armswings in the game. Oddly enough, however, he followed through with his elbow bent in a recoil fashion behind his left ear—a rare irregularity among superstars. Despite his keen competitive spirit, Bohn experienced a decline in his game. Having coached him occasionally over the years, I advised him to abandon his aggressive, behind-the-ear follow-through in favor of a softer, extended one. I feel certain that, armed with a less aggressive follow-through, Bohn will regain his magic touch.

Parker Bohn III changed to a softer, extended follow-through.

Correcting the Follow-Through Styles of Steve Hoskins, Amleto Monacelli, and Tim Criss

Steve Hoskins joined the tour in 1989, and, like many of the aforementioned players, he exerted excessive force in his follow-through. Although he was selected Rookie of the Year, he was erratic in spare conversions and failed to emerge victorious in his first 3 years on tour. He sought my advice in 1993. My first objective was to temper his follow-through. We started by suppressing his forearm thrust and emphasizing a greater swing from the shoulder. Without sacrificing any power, he softened his delivery slightly, eliminated a major portion of his forearm action, and completed his follow-through with his arm fully extended outward. Two weeks later, Hoskins notched his first PBA title at Grand Prairie, Texas. Following this dramatic change, he annexed 9 additional titles, placing him in the elite 10-title fraternity.

Amleto Monacelli has recorded 19 titles and 33 perfect games and earned more than US$1.8 million. Amleto gained most of his fame prior to the advent of reactive bowling balls. He was one of the few successful players who followed through as if he were starting a lawn mower. He released the ball with incredible finger rotation and whipped his arm skyward with a bent elbow. His production fell off during the early and mid-1990s, principally due to the erratic hooking action of reactive equipment. Having coached Monacelli in his early years on tour, I suggested a softer follow-through with greater extension and minimal elbow bend. He assumed greater control, and the results were astounding. He had a better read on the ball and succeeded in harnessing all his power to great advantage.

For many years, Tim Criss was a journeyman on the PBA Tour. Though he was one of the hardest-working players on tour, practicing diligently night after night, he was rarely a threat; more often than not, he ended up a spectator. In the late 1990s, he heeded my advice, abandoned his behind the ear follow-through in favor of a longer extension, and became an overnight success.

During a PBA Tour practice session in the 2002–2003 season, I was coaching Gene McCune, who was accompanied by Steve Jaros, a fellow Illinoisan. Jaros asked if I had any suggestions for improving his game. While not as successful as Bohn, Jaros also followed through in a recoil manner, with his elbow bent behind his ear. I informed Jaros that this technique had proved counterproductive with the explosive modern balls, producing sharp-hooking, often uncontrollable shots. I recommended a softer, outward extension of his follow-though and worked with him for

Steve Jaros demonstrates his follow-through: *(a)* the recoil method he used early in his career was counterproductive; *(b)* a softer, extended follow-through is more productive.

the remainder of that practice session, as well as numerous others during the rest of the season. The repetitious workouts brought about remarkable results that transformed Jaros from journeyman to elite bowler. During the following season, he captured three titles and won more than US$166,000.

A bumper crop of outstanding amateurs joined the PBA in 1998, including Chris Barnes, Patrick Healey Jr., Rudy Kasimakis, Kurt Pilon, and Robert Smith. Unsurprisingly, all possessed ideal follow-throughs. Barnes, a former Wichita State star and Team USA member, has been the most successful of the class of '98. He recorded two titles in his sophomore season and is a threat in every tournament he enters. Barnes uses a fluid follow-through that delivers power through the fingers instead of the forearm.

Robert Smith delivers the most powerful strike balls on tour. He performs with minimal effort, releasing low and long and with minimal elbow bend.

In the event that some bowling scholars, coaches, or instructors disagree with my theories on proper follow-through, please do not misconstrue this method of execution as flimsy, fragile, or weak. Soft, as interpreted

Perfecting the Follow-Through

Mistake	Modification
1. Ball is lofted upward onto the lane.	**1.** Deliver the ball into the lane.
2. Elbow is bent and arm is recoiled in a violent manner.	**2.** Keep arm extended with minimal elbow bend. Do this by driving the fingers to the breakpoint—no higher, no lower. The weight of the ball and the flow of the swing will produce a slight bend in the elbow on the follow-through. It must be natural, not forced or exaggerated.
3. Follow-through goes skyward, with the fingers left of the face (for right-handers).	**3.** Follow through 90 degrees to the target.

by this writer, is a follow-through void of excessive force—silky, velvety, and delicate, yet firm and fluid.

To sum up my suggestion for executing the ideal follow-through, keep the armswing low and long. Send the fingers to the breakpoint—no higher, no lower. The weight of the ball may carry the arm and fingers slightly above this point. Just don't exert any effort to *send* it up; a slight natural upward motion will not obstruct the ideal follow-through. Avoiding use of undue force in the delivery can also prevent early roll and preserve energy in the ball until it reaches the desired breakpoint.

Remember: Low, long, and fluid. Just let it flow, flow, flow!

Establishing Your Comfort Zone

The comfort zone is the foundation for competition at your highest level. It is the combination of a relaxed mind, correct ball position, and correct starting position. Through knowledge and practice, you can achieve these essential objectives that help put you in that special moment—the signal to begin your approach.

Being in the comfort zone can best be described as beginning your approach with tunnel vision and a state of mind exuding confidence in the task at hand. It involves the relaxation of both mind and body and makes it possible to repeat shot after shot in your best form. Relaxation must reign from the moment you pick up your ball to the moment you step up to the approach and assume your stance.

Stance

Stance is the preparation for a proper approach. It is a comfort zone that you can achieve by learning and implementing both proper ball position and proper starting position, which are the ingredients for the beginning of a high-quality execution. The comfort zone is a moment of relaxation with respect to the weight and position of the ball and proper alignment of the feet and shoulders. Consider the moment you assume a well-positioned stance to be your signal to execute a high-quality shot.

An ideal stance involves taking an erect position with your knees slightly flexed. Your weight should be evenly distributed on your feet, which should be no more than 3 inches (about 8 centimeters) apart (figure 8.1). An erect posture is an asset in executing a free armswing—that is, one that provides a great pendulum drive. A free armswing is absolutely free of muscle control; it is powered by gravity's pull on the weight of the ball. A free armswing is the soundest method of execution and thus helps the bowler maintain rhythm and consistency. (The free armswing is addressed in more detail in chapter 5.)

Ball Position

One type of ball position is recommended, but variations are available. Bowlers often deviate from standard styles because they have not received proper instruction. If, by chance, a bowler becomes successful with an unorthodox style, it is the exception, not the rule. Most serious bowlers prefer to build their game on a solid foundation and grow and adapt from there. It is wise to emulate the majority of bowlers, past and present, who have achieved superstar status by performing in textbook fashion.

Figure 8.1 Chris Barnes illustrates a well-balanced stance, with *(a)* weight evenly distributed and *(b)* knees slightly flexed.

Textbook Ball Position

In textbook ball position, the elbows rest close to the hips (figure 8.2). The ball is nested in the right palm, principally supported by the left hand about waist-high and slightly right of the center of the body (for right-handed bowlers; opposite for left-handers). Use a soft upward pushaway and completely relax all muscles to allow the ball to descend into the backswing due solely to gravity's pull on the ball's weight. Maintain a comfortable ball position before the pushaway. The placement of the ball must permit an easy, undeterred pushaway.

Right-handed bowlers with average to large hips can hold the ball slightly to the right of the hips in order to eliminate the need for a circled backswing. (The circled backswing curls around the buttocks and necessitates realignment to keep the swing line closer to the body.) This placement was developed and popularized by American Bowling Congress Hall of Famer Therm Gibson. Holding the ball to the right can also be useful for bowlers who do not have average to large hips. Many slender bowlers, such

Figure 8.2 Right-hander Chris Barnes demonstrates proper ball position, with the elbows close to the hips and the ball held slightly right of the center of the body.

as PBA star Chris Barnes, also hold the ball to the right and demonstrate flawless armswings. Use whatever position that allows your ball to go into the downswing and fall into place directly in line with your body.

Naturally, the foregoing suggestions apply to women as they do to men. The average woman's hips are proportionately wider than the average man's hips; consequently, a woman more likely needs to hold her ball slightly to the right to accomplish the free armswing. Marion Ladewig, generally regarded as the greatest female bowler of all time, had a slender figure yet held the ball slightly to the right and possessed one of the most direct armswings in bowling history. Carolyn Dorin-Ballard and Wendy Macpherson, two of the top female players in America, also accomplish exemplary straight armswings by holding the ball slightly to the right, as demonstrated by Clara Guerrero in figure 8.3.

Figure 8.3   Clara Guerrero positions the ball slightly to the right of her hips to produce a free armswing.

Variations on Textbook Ball Position

When it comes to stance, there are as many variations as there are bowlers. Although it is important to start out by following the classic position described earlier, it is also important to make adjustments as needed. The goal is to find a position that's best for you and your game.

Remember: Comfort rules! You *must* remain relaxed. Consistency is the desired result, so it is wise to assume a stance that does not vary from shot to shot. You can achieve this goal by placing the ball in the same position at the start of each approach. You can keep it in the middle of your body or off to one side if you have wide hips. For players who are plagued with extremely high backswings, I suggest holding the ball low, with arms extended, then giving a soft upward shove to create a free fall of the ball. Holding the ball low can also be beneficial for players who experience difficulty due to muscling the ball into the backswing. Regardless of the positioning of the ball in the stance, the forearm of the bowling arm must remain completely relaxed.

The position of the hand at setup is irrelevant in producing the amount of hook or type of roll you are trying to achieve. This maneuver must be set at the top of the backswing, prior to beginning the forward swing. Nonetheless, one of the most helpful tips for maintaining consistency is to keep the elbows nested into your hips, regardless of how high or low you start the pushaway.

Classic players (in the sense that they perform in textbook fashion) such as Chris Barnes, Parker Bohn III, David Ozio, and Brian Voss hold the ball close to the body, slightly above the waist, with elbows at the sides firmly entrenched against the hips. It must be noted that these superstars benefit greatly from placing their arms against their hips to maintain consistency in their pushaways.

Mike Aulby employed a unique method in his starting position. His starting point was high above his head. He slowly lowered the ball to a waist-high position, then pushed up and away into a smooth, free arm-swing. Mike used this unorthodox method simply because he found this type of pushaway the most comfortable for him. It is not, however, advisable to emulate his method of execution.

Pete Weber's method contrasts with Aulby's. Pete begins his stance with the ball about chest high. He pushes the ball away in a slight upward path and pulls the ball back with an extreme tilt, thus creating an unusually high backswing. Weber acquired this method of execution by virtue of necessity. He began bowling at a very early age and, because he was small in stature, used this style to generate speed. Although Weber has perfected this technique through years of repetition, it (like Aulby's approach) is not recommended.

An erect position is both recommended and recognized as a standard, but it is not standard for everyone. Several top performers in the professional ranks have operated from a low crouch, even though this method normally prohibits a free armswing and creates the possibility of rearing up on the release. Most notably, Marshall Holman began his stance with knees slightly flexed. He bent over from the waist, lowered his arms and hands to approximately knee height (figure 8.4), and then drew the ball into the backswing. Although he controlled the ball through a short backswing, he had the uncanny ability to execute a muscle-free forward swing that depended from the shoulder. Again, this is not a recommended practice but an individual style developed by one of the greatest bowlers in the game.

Figure 8.4 Although an erect posture is recommended, Marshall Holman had great success starting from a low crouch, as demonstrated here by Danny Wiseman.

Bob Learn Jr. set up in a style similar to Holman's, with one exception: Learn bowled from a low crouch and muscled the ball into his armswing. Although he enjoyed a fair career, this method of execution places severe strain on the hand, forearm, and shoulder; as a result, it is not recommended for any aspiring bowler.

During his heyday from the 1950s into the 1970s, Hall of Famer Carmen Salvino held the ball with his elbows at his belt line and his ball about shoulder-high. His thumb was at the 1 o'clock position, well under the ball. Salvino then pushed the ball out and away and uncorked one of the most powerful balls of his era. Later in his career, Salvino altered his stance, holding the ball with his right hand fully suspended at his side and initiating his pushaway and approach by shoving the ball upward with his left hand into a ball-weighted swing. Wayne Webb adopted the Salvino style in his later years on the PBA Tour and enjoyed mild success.

Roger Bowker, a five-time PBA titlist, had one of the most unusual stances in the game. A confirmed muscle bowler, Bowker addressed the pins from an erect position with his bowling arm firmly entrenched against his hips (figure 8.5). He began his approach by pulling his ball into the

Photo courtesy of PBA, LLC.

Figure 8.5   Roger Bowker had a unique starting position.

backswing, completely muscled through the forearm, then delivered it in a similar manner throughout the forward swing. Bowker's five championships defied the logic of the free armswing theory, proving again that the sports world is sprinkled with winners who succeed despite performing against the book.

Starting Position

The approach is marked by three sets of dots (see figure 8.7 on page 137). The first set is 2 inches (5.1 centimeters) from the foul line. The next two sets are located, respectively, 12 feet (3.7 meters) and 15 feet (4.6 meters) back from the foul line. These dots on the approach serve as a guide for a starting point. The 12-foot dots are generally recommended for four-step bowlers, and the 15-foot dots are recommended for five-step players.

Determining Starting Distance From the Foul Line

Use these three steps to determine your starting position:

1. With your back to the pins, walk from the foul line to the starting position, stretching and extending the last step to simulate your slide in a normal approach.

2. Repeat the procedure in reverse: Face the pins and do your approach so that you end up near the foul line.

3. Place your starting point a few inches behind the first set of dots on the approach and do a four-step approach. Repeat this process while making any needed adjustments to place the sliding toe within a couple of inches from the foul line.

Taller bowlers are naturally inclined to take longer steps. For instance, during the mid-1980s, Del Warren, who stood 6 feet 5 inches (about 2 meters) tall, was struggling with his game. He began with his heels dangling off the approach area and took five long steps to the foul line in a robotic manner, with no visible rhythm or timing. He sought my help, and I immediately altered his stance by moving him all the way up to the first set of dots on the approach. I also changed his approach from five steps to four and shortened his steps by half their length. Within an hour, Warren developed one of the smoothest approaches on tour. (See his story in chapter 4.)

Generally, a shorter, quicker pace is far more advantageous than longer, calculated steps in establishing a rhythmic approach. This subject is addressed in more detail in chapter 4.

Perfecting the Stance

Mistake	Modification
1. Body is too rigid.	1. Relax the body by taking deep breaths.
2. Knees are locked.	2. Bend knees slightly to release tension in the lower body.
3. Back is arched.	3. Do not arch back. This places the body in an awkward alignment.
4. Toes, shoulders, and body are not aligned to the target area.	4. Align toes, hips, and shoulders.

Aligning Feet and Shoulders to Target

The cardinal rule for proper bowling execution is this: The bowling arm *must* follow the line of the body, regardless of the angle of the shot. Proper alignment *always* begins with the shoulders and feet, which must be directly in line with the desired target. In other words, face your target. The feet determine the path of the approach. Any misdirection of the feet can be disastrous. Picture a fire truck driven by two steering mechanisms—one driving the front wheels, the other maneuvering the rear wheels. If the front driver makes a right turn and the rear driver does not correspond, the result is chaos.

In determining how far left or right you want to position your feet at the start of the approach, you can use the left big toe, the right big toe, or the instep to mark the desired position. Some bowlers place the center of the toe on a certain board; others measure the boards with the inner part of the foot. There is no specific standard of measurement. As long as it is a set pattern, it should work for you. The primary rule is to align the toes and shoulders to the target.

For right-handers, any attempt to swing the ball to an area outside the 2nd arrow (opposite for left-handers), with the shoulder line perpendicular and feet parallel to the foul line, results in pulling the shot. Lining up for a strike shot is similar to taking a stance for a 7-pin or 10-pin conversion. You move to a cross-lane position and walk in that direction. Any attempt to address these corner pins with the shoulder line and feet parallel to the foul line will result in a blown spare.

Point your feet and shoulders in a direct line to the intended target with utter disregard for your alignment in relation to the foul line. For example, when you are playing the 2nd arrow, down and in, the right shoulder must align with the 10th board (figure 8.6a). When you're playing a deep inside angle (in which the ball is laid down on the 25th board at the foul line to reach a breakpoint at the 10th board), the feet, torso, and shoulder must be aligned in that direction (figure 8.6b). The breakpoint is the area on the lane where the ball begins its entry to the pocket. It is 15 feet (4.6 meters) from the 1-3 pocket for a right-handed bowler and the same distance from the 1-2 pocket for left-handed bowlers. In bowling jargon, this is referred to as *opening up the lane.* All shots should be performed with the arm and torso squared to the desired mark. Anything else will result in misdirection or a pull in the armswing.

Not only is it advantageous to spot a target from the foul line to the arrows, but, as many top players do, it also helps to draw an imaginary line from the arrows to the breakpoint, as shown in figure 8.7. As high-powered bowling balls have made the breakpoint easier to predict, this method of alignment has become standard. Although the arrows are the targets for determining the ball's path toward the pins, the breakpoint plays a major role in determining strike percentage.

Figure 8.6 Danny Wiseman aligns his right shoulder *(a)* with the 10th board for a down-and-in shot and *(b)* with the 25th board to play a deep inside angle.

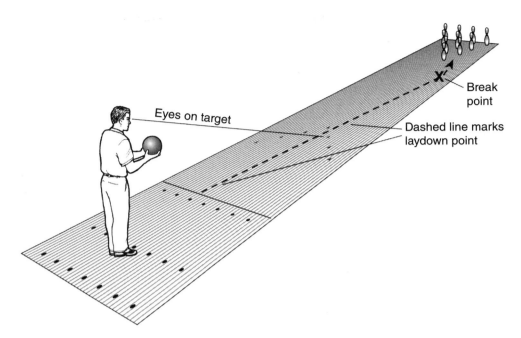

Figure 8.7 A good method of alignment is to spot a target from the foul line to the arrows, then draw an imaginary line from the target board to the breakpoint.

Comfortable and Rhythmic Approach

When aiming to establish a preshot comfort zone, remember that relaxation is the key. During foul shot attempts, professional basketball players display one of the most practical forms of relaxation. Notice that many players bounce the ball several times, take a deep breath, exhale, and then immediately flip the ball toward the hoop. In this manner, the muscles are free of tension. I use the terms *tension-free* and *comfortable* throughout my coaching and throughout this book. After coaching sessions with me, many students profess how effortless it is to bowl game after game and never tire. Those who experienced chronic aches and pains while bowling were relieved of such discomforts after using the techniques I espouse. Enjoy the sport. Keep your body in proper alignment. Let physics and gravity, not muscle, do all the work for you.

Step Up, Line Up, and Go!

Apply the analogy of basketball players as they execute free throws; again, they set themselves, take a deep breath, exhale, and then immediately shoot the ball. It should be the same in bowling. Taking too much time is often detrimental, since it usually creates undesired tension. How often have you had a great game yet fallen short of the marks you deserve and desire? Great bowlers such as Chris Barnes, Parker Bohn III, Norm Duke, Pete Weber, and Walter Ray Williams spend minimal time in their stance. They select their starting position, line up their feet, and start their approach. You can do the same. Pick your starting point, face your target, take a deep breath, exhale, and start your approach without delay. One of my best students, a PBA member, has yet to make his mark in PBA regional competition despite the fact that he possesses an outstanding physical game. To date, he has failed to overcome the tension that mounts as he overprepares on the approach. My advice, to borrow a slogan, is "Just do it!"

Approach Habits of the Pros

Ball positioning and proper alignment of the feet and shoulders constitute the physical aspects of a proper stance, but we need to remember that there is also a mental aspect. A bowler must take the stance with a clear mind.

Although fundamentals developed through muscle memory become ingrained, this is no assurance that all systems are go. Despite seemingly complete preparation, numerous bowlers have developed idiosyncrasies that set them apart from others, and some of the PBA's most seasoned veterans have quirky lapses in their stances. The most prominent one who comes to mind is Barry Asher, one of the greatest talents ever to grace the professional ranks. Although Asher racked up 10 national titles in an abbreviated career, he reached a period when he had extreme difficulty in starting his approach. He would rock back and forth, stutter, back off—as many as three to six times. He could not motivate his feet into the approach. No matter how hard he tried, nothing seemed to help.

On a flight home after a PBA tournament that he lost by one 10-pin, Asher picked up a sport magazine that featured a psychologist who was also a hypnotist. The sport psychologist's clients included top names in all sports. Upon arriving home, he made an appointment with this psychologist for the next day. Asher made more than 35 visits, yet he was unable to overcome his problem. He did manage to win eight more titles, but the problem became so distressing that he chose to retire from the PBA Tour in the prime of his career. In my opinion, this is one of the most tragic stories in PBA history.

Asher bowled league and senior tournaments years later, but never returned to the regular tour. In 1985, he captured the ABC All-Events crown, but because of his inability to keep pace, his team finished bowling 90 minutes later than the other teams. At any rate, Barry's All-Events title qualified him for the U.S. team in the FIQ world competition in England. (FIQ stands for Fédération Internationale des Quilleurs, or International Bowling Federation.) Barry, easily the best bowler on the American team, continued to be plagued by his inability to start his approach and was asked to withdraw from the competition. To this day, he continues to experience difficulty in starting his approach.

Bad habits, particularly those created by mental blocks, are seemingly impossible to break. Yet some people manage to move on in spite of them.

PBA Hall of Fame member George Pappas was also notorious for peculiar characteristics in his stance. Unquestionably one of the best clutch bowlers in the game, Pappas was cool under fire and a virtual cinch to strike in crucial situations. Nevertheless, while addressing pins in his stance, he took excessive time in starting his approach. He developed a habit of twisting and rolling his shoulders, repeating this seemingly nervous twitch two or three times and consuming 20 to 25 seconds before placing the ball into the pushaway. Pappas won 10 titles, including the Firestone Tournament of Champions. After his retirement from the regular PBA Tour, Pappas became a successful proprietor, and he occasionally takes time off to compete on the Senior Tour with great success.

Ernie Schlegel was the slowest bowler on the PBA Tour. Perhaps that could have been attributed to his excessive readiness. Schlegel went through a series of mental preparations while he addressed the pins. He took such excessive time in televised events that the PBA was forced to pass a rule requiring bowlers to begin their approach within 25 seconds or face a US$25 fine for each violation.

Mark Roth, recently honored as one of the top 20 bowlers of the 20th century by *ABC Bowling Magazine,* took little or no time to go into action. His incredible record belies the old adage that "haste makes waste." Roth picked up his ball, looked down at his starting position, and raced without hesitation to the foul line—all to the tune of 34 PBA national titles!

Proper bowling execution is based on the coordination of arms and feet in flowing motion. This coordination is the key to precise timing. Focus on the job at hand, exhale, and, without hesitation, take the first step. Activate your movements in rhythm and execute the entire process until the release point. Through knowledge and practice, you can achieve that special moment—your signal to begin your approach.

Fine-Tuning Your Game

In all fields of sport, participants who strive for perfection adhere to specific standards in order to maintain a competitive edge. They practice diligently, stay well-conditioned, and place their confidence in qualified coaches.

The old adage "practice makes perfect" can, at times, be an exaggeration. You may recall the joke about an aspiring musician who was lost in New York City. He came upon a hippie and inquired, "How do you get to Carnegie Hall?" The hippie replied, "Practice, man. Practice." Although studiously practicing one's craft demonstrates a great work ethic and is undoubtedly a worthwhile pursuit, it can be detrimental if it isn't done properly, particularly in bowling. Practice must be done properly in order to benefit your game.

A successful bowler who is in the groove is executing properly and duplicating correct movements. For those who are experiencing difficulty, however, rehearsing deficiencies that have crept into their games will only intensify and prolong their agony.

At its highest level, bowling is an intricate sport. Seemingly great shots in bowling often result in negative results such as 4-pins, 7-pins, 8-pins, and 10-pins. Many of these single-pin leaves result from release flaws that are too difficult for the average bowler to detect with the naked eye. Only eagle-eyed bowlmasters can detect inferior releases and release points, and these experts are precisely the people you should turn to for help in correcting your mistakes. To establish your goals, seek out a qualified coach or perhaps a teammate who understands your game.

Proper bowling execution incorporates several principles; although they are separate, they must be blended into a smooth, rhythmic manner. These are the principles involved:

- ✗ Stance (body position)
- ✗ Pushaway
- ✗ Free armswing
- ✗ Footwork (approach)
- ✗ Knee bend
- ✗ Hand position and release
- ✗ Follow-through

The following instructions are presented for right-handed bowlers; turn them around if you're a left-hander.

Assume a Relaxed Stance

The stance, or the body position at the start of the approach, must be free of tension. Comfort rules! There are no set standards. Many bowlers feel comfortable in erect positions, whereas others feel content in semicrouched positions. Either is acceptable—as long as you are relaxed and comfortable. The main objective is to assume a position that enables you to begin your approach to the foul line with no restrictions.

Various coaches and instructors differ on stance. I prefer the erect position because I'm a firm believer in a free armswing delivered from the shoulder joint, and an erect position permits a freer flow of the arm than a lower or crouched position can enable. Many PBA stars begin in an erect position. Most notable in this respect are Chris Barnes, David Ozio, Brian Voss, and Walter Ray Williams. It is important to note that all of these players exercise a long, free armswing initiated from a smooth pushaway.

In contrast, witness the great successes of Norm Duke and Danny Wiseman, who start their approaches from a crouch. It may or may not be coincidental, but both of these players are small in stature. Each employs a semicontrolled armswing yet has the innate ability to relax the arm in the downswing.

Walter Ray Williams uses an erect position in the initial stance.

Don't Force the Pushaway

The pushaway is one of the most vital maneuvers in proper bowling execution. As with stance, the pushaway can involve optional features. Players who operate from a low crouch generally apply a semicontrolled swing, and the majority of bowlers in this category use a lower, outward pushaway and partially control the ball into the backswing.

Fundamentally, however, an ideal pushaway is one in which the ball is pushed slightly upward and then allowed to respond to gravitational pull. This type of pushaway must not be exaggerated or performed too forcefully. Although one's grip in the ball should be firm, the pushaway is soft and delicate, just sufficiently arced to permit the ball to free-fall into the backswing.

Patrick Allen's fundamentally sound pushaway.

David Ozio and Brian Voss possess the soundest fundamentals in bowling. They execute model pushaways—extended, delicate, unforced, and consistent. Initiating their games with this classic pushaway helps them remain among the smoothest players in the game.

Mike Aulby's incredible success can also be attributed to his superb pushaway. On occasions, however, Mike tends to tilt in the pushaway. The key to eliminating this flaw is to maintain the shoulders in the upright position. Do not follow the pushaway with the shoulders. This is a common error, and it was one of the few flaws in Aulby's game that I focused on during the 20-some years for which I coached him. Nevertheless, it didn't prevent him from winning close to 30 titles, including all 5 major events: the PBA National (twice), the Touring Players Championship, the BPAA U.S. Open, the Tournament of Champions, and the ABC Masters (three times). No other player in the history of the game has won all 5 majors.

Adopt a Straight, Free Armswing

The term *armswing* refers to the manner in which the arm travels from the pushaway to the release point. Leading instructors and coaches have varied opinions on proper armswing. Many players—particularly power players—push the ball away to the left, walk to the left, open up their shoulders to the target, and then unleash wide-arcing hooks. This is the pattern for modern players who delight in opening up the lanes by swinging from a deep inside angle to the outer part of the lanes. It is effective when lanes are dry on the outside, since it permits the ball to enter at a wide angle and create a greater strike percentage. With modern equipment, though, it can result in some of the weirdest splits imaginable.

Many notable coaches recommend the figure-8 swing or a modified figure-8. In a true figure-8, the ball is swung into the pushaway with the hand under the ball. As the ball is approximately three-quarters of the way into the backswing, the thumb of the hand turns down and in to the left, then reverses its movement back to the right and under the ball, actually forming a figure-8 as it begins its descent into the forward swing. Years ago, the figure-8 was a common maneuver among star players. The modern method (for right-handed players, opposite for left-handers) starts the pushaway toward the left of the body, forcing the swing to bump out to the right, away from the body. As the arm reaches the top of the swing, the arm and hand form a half-figure-8, then veer back toward the body line, descending in a straight path. The objective is to keep the hand under and inside the ball.

During the early 1940s, Ned Day was one of the original figure-8 bowlers. The Milwaukee star was one of the most artistic bowlers of his era—smooth as silk, perfectly balanced, and seemingly flawless. Day was the classic figure-8 bowler. Don Johnson, one of the most dominant PBA players in the 1970s, was a semi-figure-8 player. Johnson's backswing was straight as an arrow. He began his figure-8 on the forward swing and applied it solely through the hand down to the release point. (His follow-through, however, took a different course.) Wayne Zahn, another star of the 1960s and 1970s, used the same type of swing that Johnson did, with one particular exception: his follow-through.

The figure-8 swing is a matter of preference, but it does present a possible stumbling block. It involves excessive movement in the backswing and thus necessitates realignment. I firmly recommend the straight armswing simply because it eliminates inordinate movements that necessitate adjustment. If armswings following an inside–outside course are not properly adjusted, one of two mistakes can occur:

1. The ball squirts to the right.
2. Improper realignment results in a pulled shot to the left.

An outside–inside swing also necessitates realignment; otherwise it will follow a natural course to the Brooklyn side of the pocket (for right-handed bowlers, opposite for left-handers).

With all due respect to bowlers, amateur or professional, whose arm-swings necessitate realignment, I strongly recommend an armswing that follows a straight path from the pushaway into the backswing and continues through the forward swing, concluding with a *straight,* extended follow-through.

Carry Out a Balanced, Rhythmic Approach

The term *footwork* refers to the pattern of your steps in the approach, and pacing the approach is one of the most important elements in proper execution. It is the basic foundation for rhythm and timing—two ingredients vital to pinpointing your release. Improper tempo results in either early or irregular late swings.

Unfortunately, in various areas of coaching and instruction, many students and advanced bowlers aren't receiving good information. For example, many bowlers who do not drift in their approach (i.e., those who walk in a straight line) are instructed to slide on the same board on which they began their approach. This is a serious error in judgment. The sliding step *must* finish directly in line with the preceding step, the power step, which is the third step in a four-step approach or the fourth step in a five-step approach. When you slide in line with the power step, your hips are cleared for the descent of the forward swing, and your swing stays close to your body to prevent the flying elbow. This approach also aids in avoiding a pulled shot. Equally as important, this maneuver forms a tripod for balancing the body. If your sliding foot does not move in under the previous step, the right side of your body, coupled with the weight of the ball, creates an imbalance, causing you to fall to the right. In doing so, you misdirect the ball. This strategy isn't confined to those who walk in a straight path. Bowlers who drift to the right or left must adhere to the same system: Slide in line with the previous step.

The ideal cadence in foot patterns permits the slide to arrive at the foul line a fraction of a second before the release point. This technique allows you to be firmly planted, wait for the swing to descend to its flat plane, and then release the ball at its greatest leverage position.

Bend the Knee for a Low Release

The knee bend is one of the requisites in proper bowling execution. It was the most positive factor for Don Carter, acknowledged by the Bowling Writers Association of America as one of the three greatest players of all time. Carter used a crouched position and shuffled to the foul line with his nose seemingly to the ground. He kept his elbow bent throughout the swing and practically pushed the ball down the lane. In fact, Carter made his approach in a manner totally opposite of the fundamentals, except for one important factor—his knee bend, which made him one of the most accurate shotmakers in the game.

Michael Haugen uses a deep knee bend to deliver the ball low into the lane.

Although a deep knee bend is generally the most important element in releasing the ball into the lane from a low position, several PBA bowlers have done very well without deep knee bends. Two examples are Dave Ferraro and Ryan Shafer. Ferraro, now retired from the Tour, won nine titles, despite the fact that he retired in his prime. Ryan Shafer came into his own in 2000 and 2001, won three titles, and became one of the top five performers in the game. Although Ferraro and Shafer have almost no knee bend, both release the ball in a downward trajectory—that is, into the lane rather than upward onto the lane. For most bowlers, the deep knee bend, which provides a low release of the ball into the lane, generally provides the best result.

Opinions conflict among some bowling instructors regarding proper knee bend. Although justifiable emphasis is placed on bending during the sliding step, we must underscore the step preceding the slide—the power step, which is the most meaningful step of the entire exercise. (The following information assumes a four-step approach for right-handed bowlers; left-handed bowlers would do the opposite.) The power step is the catalyst for descending into a slide, which enables a bowler to release the ball from a low angle. The power step is used to push off into the slide in a low, firm position, which also prevents the body from rearing up at the line.

A deep knee bend in the third step of a four-step delivery can be more effective if it is short and rapid. This permits a bowler to descend more easily into a sitting position. A long third step will hinder any attempt to take a seat, creating a block in the knee bend and resulting in the bowler's rearing up after the initial slide.

A deep knee bend is the trademark of numerous current PBA stars, such as Chris Barnes, Parker Bohn III, Tommy Delutz Jr., Norm Duke, Steve Jaros, Tommy Jones, Wes Malott, Sean Rash, Tony Reyes, Pete Weber, and Walter Ray Williams. It was also the strong suit for past bowling greats Ray Bluth, Don Johnson, Dick Ritger, and Jim Stefanich. Marshall Holman, recently honored by *ABC Magazine* as one of the 20 greatest bowlers of the century, attained his lofty standing by virtue of a deep knee bend that allowed him to finish in a low, outward path.

Mike Aulby, despite his incredible record, had one chink in his armor. Though his record seems to refute the importance of a good knee bend, Aulby was prone to occasional slumps due to his sporadic failure to descend on his power step. In coaching Aulby during the past 20 years, I focused on this area of his game. Aulby was not alone among successful players on the PBA Tour. Others who did not execute textbook knee bends include Justin Hromek, Bob Learn Jr., Butch Soper, and David Traber; all fared well in the pro ranks despite their inability to execute ideal knee bends. Ryan Shafer, another of the more successful players on the current PBA Tour, has also benefitted from a rather short stature, an advantage that has permitted him to release the ball from a low position.

Again, I relate the exceptions, yet I always want to state the rule: A deep knee bend is generally one of the requisites for proper execution.

Wait for the Proper Release Point

A strong release is the envy of all bowlers. Many great players are blessed with this talent, others develop the desired release through study and practice, and some are simply unable to master this important point of execution. Nonetheless, many bowlers achieve great success by relying on accuracy and simplicity. A strong release involves the ability to place the ball well back in the hand and the patience to wait for the proper release point, maintaining hand position until the last moment before removing the thumb. The next element is to drive the ball off the front part of the hand into the lane with strong finger rotation.

During the era of rubber and polyester bowling balls, it wasn't uncommon to see good players release the ball on the upswing. Known as the *life-and-turn* technique, this method of execution was not as critical a flaw then as it is today, since balls made in the past did not have the gripping characteristics of today's modern missiles.

For those not naturally inclined to it, coordinating the release at the proper release point can be quite difficult. This practice involves movements that demand split-second synchronization. They go together or go nowhere. A great release at the improper release point is counterproductive.

The ideal release point is an area at or a little behind the ankle during the downswing. Take the thumb out, transfer the weight of the ball to the fingers, and drive the ball from the strongest leverage point. The release point should be approximately six or seven boards from the sliding foot, provided the slide is in line with the previous step.

During the 1970s and 1980s, Marshall Holman had the consummate release. It set a model for many contemporary bowlers. Holman was once featured demonstrating his technique on a slow-motion Brunswick promotional tape. His release was lightning quick, but even more impressive was the Medford Meteor's knack of seemingly laying the ball down into the lane. Holman's release featured a cupped wrist that collapsed at the release, then whipped forward through his fingers and into the lane.

Several years ago, I served as technical adviser for Marshall Holman on an instructional video, *Maximum Bowling,* which focused on fundamentals. Holman demonstrated the advantage of carrying out a superb release that corresponds with an ideal release point. The video also exposed the harmful effects of an early swing, particularly the damaging results of hitting up on the release.

Hitting up on the ball must not be confused with hitting *out* on the ball. Hitting up and lofting occur when balls are released in an upward motion and enter the lane in a bouncing fashion. Hitting *out*, in contrast, means feeding the ball into the lane, a manner of execution that has enhanced the careers of such stars as Tommy Baker, Chris Barnes, Parker Bohn III, Norm Duke, and David Ozio.

Pete Weber, a great pure talent, has one of the cleanest releases ever. It appears effortless, yet it is among the most explosive strike balls in the sport. Like Holman, Weber lays the ball into the lane smoothly, with no sound or bounce whatsoever. Holman and Weber confirm that excessive force and raw power are not necessary for a strong release; rather, it is exact timing, delivered delicately, that is essential. Weber can best be described as a power stroker, and though he exemplifies the power stroke he isn't alone in using this type of game.

There are two other categories of releases: pure strokers and crankers with raw power. The pure strokers include Chris Barnes, Parker Bohn III, Tommy Jones, Doug Kent, and Wes Malott. They rely on finesse and pinpoint accuracy.

Crankers rely not on finesse but on raw power. They apply extreme wrist and finger rotation to create excessive revolutions. They are less exacting than strokers and use their talents to create a wider pocket; that is, they deliver the ball to a specific area rather than to a certain board. Power players are far more effective when the lanes afford wider angles to the pocket—angles that present a tremendous advantage in strike percentage. Power crankers are practically unbeatable when conditions favor their game. The most notable crankers on the PBA Tour are Jason Couch (who is great on all conditions), Brian Himmler, Brian Kretzer, Sean Rash, and Robert Smith.

Extend Your Follow-Through Outward, Not Upward

Equally important is the motion of the arm after the release—the all-important follow-through, which is one of the most significant mechanical elements in sports. You see it in baseball, football, basketball, billiards, track and field, tennis, and golf. It is the culmination of most motions that require the arms and legs.

Improper follow-through has been an Achilles heel for baseball pitchers since the game began. They develop sore arms, are beset by control problems, hang curveballs, lose speed and movement on their fastballs, and slide into funks when they exercise their follow-through improperly. Basketball players who excel at long-range shooting rely on a delicate follow-through to make shots. Golfers who drive balls in the 300-yard (275-meter) range would be ordinary mortals but for crisp and undeterred follow-throughs, and improper follow-throughs on putting greens have been the bane of many pros.

An inferior follow-through has hampered many bowlers as well. This problem derives in part from the various methods being taught in today's game. As a practicing coach and instructor, I find it disconcerting to be

Professionals vary in their follow-throughs: *(a)* Steve Jaros demonstrates an old-style follow-through, reaching for the ceiling; *(b)* Brenda Mack directs the follow-through out toward the pins.

critical of other teachers. However, because of modern trends in bowling equipment and lane maintenance, the physical aspect of the game has evolved.

The fundamentals are still the cornerstones for proper execution. Nevertheless, one of the most flagrant errors occurring in today's game involves the follow-through. This common flaw is an unfortunate carryover from the days of old rubber balls and shellac and lacquer finishes. These conditions demanded aggressiveness in the release and follow-through, and players were taught to lift and turn the ball and to reach for the ceiling on their follow-through. Now, however, the game features bowling balls made of materials that generate greater friction on the lanes. Manufacturers are no longer confined to making old pancake blocks that merely serve to counterbalance the weight removed in drilling. Research and development geniuses spend hundreds of thousands of dollars developing sophisticated weight blocks that are placed in strategic areas of the ball for additional power. Also, educated drillers are now able to place weight blocks in such a manner that they can virtually control hook patterns in any ball, on any condition, and at any desired breakpoint.

In this era of active, reactive, and proactive equipment, overly aggressive follow-throughs that head skyward are detrimental to a bowler. Modern balls require the bowler to use more finesse, and a moderately stroked ball is far more effective than one delivered too aggressively. This is true because of the gripping characteristics of modern missiles that result in overreaction: Balls with excessive revolutions tend to hook too sharply, whereas those delivered more delicately move in a gradual arc.

Power bowlers Buddy Bomar, Dick Hoover, Bill Lillard, Carmen Salvino, and Harry Smith applied the old style of follow-through (lift and turn and reach for the ceiling) and were extremely successful. Nonetheless, many great bowlers defied this logic and directed their follow-throughs out toward the pins. Bowlers such as Don Carter, Tom Hennessey, Joe Joseph, Junie McMahon, and Billy Welu all ended their deliveries toward the pins.

Thunderous upward follow-throughs cause the ball to spin while airborne. As a result, the ball reacts immediately on contact with the lane. In contrast, a ball delivered low and out toward the pins is more likely to undergo the textbook action that bowlers seek: skid, roll, and hook.

One of the best components of a proper follow-through is the softening extension of the fingers and arm. The fingers extend outward, *not* upward, to the breakpoint. Make a concentrated effort to keep the arm extended, with little or no bend in the elbow. You can accomplish this only if you deliver the swing from the shoulder; any delivery generated from the forearm prevents proper follow-through.

My position regarding proper follow-through is supported by comments from two astute students of the game. Earl Anthony subscribed to this theory: Follow the ball with your hand. Tom Kouros, one of the greatest coaches in the game, recalls some sage advice from all-time great Junie McMahon: Direct your follow-through to the pins; they are down there. McMahon, pointing to the pin deck, told Kouros, "When they place them up in the ceiling, you can direct your follow-through up there."

Armed with these words of wisdom from such bowling luminaries regarding this phase of the game, I highly recommend a softer, longer, extended follow-through as part of the ideal execution and as one of the seven steps to success in bowling.

A high-quality follow-through can enhance your game in several ways. It plays an integral role in maintaining proper balance, and it is advantageous in mastering ball reaction. Excessive vigor in the follow-through—particularly, inordinate force generated from the elbow—greatly affects the hooking pattern of the ball on its path to the pocket.

Opening Up
the Lanes

Modern bowling balls have given a new meaning to the popular phrase "opening up the lanes," which refers to the widening of the track, or area, that the ball covers on its path to the pocket. However, bowlers who delight in opening up the lanes must remember another popular adage—"the shortest distance between two points is a straight line"—and learn to beat conditions that are extremely dry, particularly in the heads or front part of the lane. This condition constitutes a sensitive predicament for players who rely on wide-arcing deliveries. More generally, how you go about opening up the lanes depends on what type of bowler you are.

Categories of Bowlers

Let's identify the strokers, power strokers, power players, and straight players on the PBA Tour as examples of opening up the lanes.

Strokers

Strokers are identified by their soft, flowing armswings and impeccable approaches. They achieve optimal power with minimal effort. They are picturesque and perfectly balanced, and they personify the textbook manner of execution. History suggests that strokers have a big advantage in the PBA. Witness the tremendous success and longevity of current players Tommy Baker, Chris Barnes, Parker Bohn III, Tommy Delutz Jr.,

Norm Duke, Steve Jaros, Tommy Jones, Doug Kent, Wes Malott, and Mike Scroggins.

Even so, the task of opening up the lanes may be a challenge for the average stroker, who employs a smooth, undeterred, free armswing with a slight acceleration at the release point. This style may encourage a stroker to exert abnormal arm speed to drive the ball through the dry area rather than permit the ball to flow through the entire delivery. A flowing follow-through must not be mistaken for a weak delivery. In fact, top-rated strokers, particularly players on the PBA circuit, may not generate as much energy into the pins as power players do, but they can compensate and produce as great a strike percentage as power players by lessening the entry angle to the pocket.

Power Strokers

Power strokers closely resemble pure strokers, with two exceptions. First, like power players (addressed next), power strokers drift leftward (for right-handers; rightward for left-handers), open up their shoulders, and then realign their bodies on their deliveries. Second, they apply greater revolutions to the ball than do pure strokers. Although they exert more effort in their releases, they manage to maintain a flowing pattern in their follow-throughs. Thus power strokers combine a stroker's minimal effort with a cranker's wider angle to the pocket. This category includes Jeff Carter, Mike DeVaney, and Pete Weber. Tim Criss would fit in either category. He combines great finger rotation with what may be the slowest ball on tour.

Power Players

These players epitomize the word *power*. They deliver explosive missiles powered by extraordinary finger and wrist rotation. They sacrifice accuracy and create a greater area, and they can be dominant on conditions that favor their wide-arcing balls. Pure power players exert far more effort than power strokers do. Because bowlers who play the power game—including Dave D'Entremont, Brian Himmler, Tommy Jones, Brian Kretzer, Sean Rash, and Robert Smith—rely on extreme wrist and finger movement for excessive revolutions, they are far more comfortable covering wider angles. Power players and some power strokers use the entire lane, but there is one major dissimilarity between them: Pure power players expend greater energy and apply excessive torque and speed to achieve their goals.

Straight Shooters

Walter Ray Williams and Norm Duke are the premier straight shooters on the PBA Tour. Their method of attacking pins is far superior to those of other straight players, because, in their path to the pocket, their balls maintain drive through the pins without the deflection factor that normally plagues straight players.

Straight players seldom play inside the 17th board and rarely, if ever, attempt to deliver the ball against the grain. Williams has mastered the end-over-end roll and, although he isn't as proficient in applying rotation to the ball when conditions dictate the tactic, he still manages to do well. Williams' end-over-end roll has propelled him to more than 40 titles and branded him as the most dominant player of the 1990s. (Williams has earned close to US$4 million in his PBA career.) Other PBA stars who rely on an accurate, straighter shot have not fared as well. Roger Bowker, Ernie Schlegel, Dave Traber, and the now-retired Butch Soper managed to make a living playing a direct line to the pocket, but this group is hardly among the elite. In 33 years as a pro, Schlegel has collected only six titles, and the rest haven't fared any better. In 27 years as a pro, Soper also had only six titles. Bowker, also a 27-year PBA veteran, owns five titles. In 17 years as a pro, Traber has recorded four championships. Another retired PBA member, Curtis Odom, knocked on the door several times in his 19-year stint as a PBA member, yet never recorded a national title. With the exception of Walter Ray Williams, straight shooters appear to be at a disadvantage when compared with those who angle their shots into the pocket.

Methods for Opening Up the Lanes

Opening the lanes requires a lay-down point (the board on which the ball is released) anywhere from the 30th to the 40th board for a right-handed bowler. The ball crosses a section of the lane somewhere between the 4th and 6th arrows and reaches a breakpoint between the 5th and 10th boards. This technique is referred to as *bellying the ball*.

This maneuver can be achieved in various ways, depending on the amount of oil dressing on the lane, which dictates certain numerical combinations for driving the ball into the pocket. These combinations are derived by a minus and plus system relating to the board of the slide foot at the point of delivery, the board at the arrows, and the breakpoint from which the ball arcs or angles into the pocket. For example, to increase the angle to the pocket, shift your feet left one board and move your target one board to the left (for a right-hander). If your desired breakpoint is not satisfactory, increase the movements to the right or left until you achieve the right results. In bowling jargon, these adjustments are referred to as 1-1, 2-1, and 2-2 moves; they serve to increase or decrease the angle of the ball.

Figure 10.1 illustrates the angles necessary for lane conditions that are dry and require wider angles to the pocket. Moving away from the target with a bigger hook overcomes dry lanes in which the ball tends to hook too early.

Aligning Feet and Shoulders to the Target

The most conventional method of opening the lanes is to approach and address lanes with shoulders and feet squared to the target. For example, on conditions dictating a starting point on the left portion of the lane—an area between the 25th and 40th boards (for right-handers)—PBA standouts Del Ballard Jr., Chris Barnes, Norm Duke, David Ozio, and Brian Voss address the lanes with their shoulders and feet toward the target. Although they tend to step slightly out of the ball path on the backswing, they maintain a square alignment with the desired target.

This stance is similar to one that most professionals use to shoot at the 10-pin, but there is one big difference: In addressing the 10-pin, there is no rotation of the fingers. In fact, the most proficient spare shooters flatten the shot to reduce or eliminate hooking action, then project the ball in a direct line to the corner pin. Norm Duke actually delivers a straight ball, sometimes even a back-up ball.

When strokers line up for a strike shot from a deep inside angle, in which the breakpoint is between the 7th and 10th boards, they square their shoulders in that direction; however, instead of flattening the shot as for spares, pros will arc the ball to the breakpoint and into the pocket by rotating the fingers counterclockwise.

On numerous occasions, strokers begin their approach in front of ball returns, which obstruct any leftward movement in a bowler's initial stance (for right-handed bowlers). Players whose games depend on lining up with their target stand in front of the ball return and drastically shorten their steps. Through practice and perseverance, they have mastered the art of coordinating a free swing, a firm release, and sufficient speed for achieving their goals.

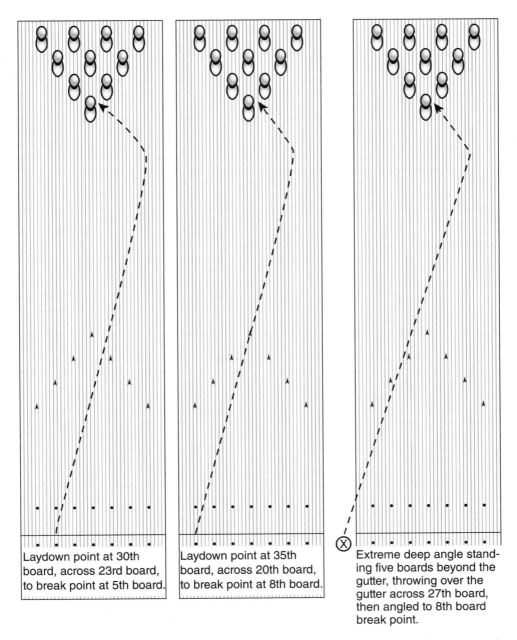

Laydown point at 30th board, across 23rd board, to break point at 5th board.

Laydown point at 35th board, across 20th board, to break point at 8th board.

Extreme deep angle standing five boards beyond the gutter, throwing over the gutter across 27th board, then angled to 8th board break point.

Figure 10.1 To overcome dry lane conditions, bowlers can move away from the target and use a bigger hook.

Shifting the Body and Realigning With the Target

Power players, particularly those who want to open up the lanes, subscribe to a different theory when ball returns prevent extreme starting positions. Some of today's players walk a straight line alongside the ball return, shift the feet and torso in front of the ball return, open their shoulders, and then realign with the intended target. Conventional wisdom suggests that this rapid shifting of feet, torso, and shoulders—along with the ensuing realignment to the target—would be extremely difficult to perform consistently. Nevertheless, a select number of PBA players are carving out a nice living using this approach. Most of these players were raised on contemporary bowling conditions and equipment. They emerged from the junior ranks and launched their careers during the urethane ball revolution. At the risk of sounding negative, I've got to say that any success achieved in walking to the left (figures 10.2*a* and 10.2*b*), shifting the feet and torso, opening up the shoulders back to the right, and delivering a ball to a specific area (figure 10.2*c*) must be regarded as an exception rather than a rule. Contemporary players who perform in this manner have become proficient through hours, days, and years of practice.

Figure 10.2 Although not recommended, some power players subscribe to the shifting and realigning approach. Here Wes Malott *(a)* starts in a straight line, *(b)* drifts to the left, and then *(c)* shifts back to the right to deliver the ball.

From an instructor's viewpoint, this is not a method of execution that warrants teaching. On the other hand, an instructor would be foolish to alter the style of anyone who has attained any degree of success. Right-handed players such as Brian Himmler, Ryan Shafer, and Pete Weber are among many PBA players who execute in this fashion.

Styles of the Pros

Pro players who use this approach—shifting and realigning to the target—have found varying degrees of success. Amleto Monacelli, an 19-time titlist, uses an open-shoulder technique. He accentuates an open position by extending his nonbowling arm forward, then drops his thumb with the palm of his hand facing the ceiling, which enables him to pull his right shoulder back, place his hand well under the ball, and thus further open his delivery. Monacelli achieved most of his victories on lanes that were conducive to wide-arcing shots, but he also notched many wins on conditions that demanded greater accuracy. The Venezuelan sharpshooter became one of the PBA's elite all-around players by virtue of his proficiency in altering hand positions and changing speeds, as well as his uncanny ability to read lanes.

Steve Hoskins emerged as one of the most successful players who specialized in opening the lanes; the stocky Floridian had 10 titles to his credit. However, his formative years on tour were mediocre at best. Although he was voted Rookie of the Year in 1989 by PBA players, he failed to win a title in his first five years. In an earlier chapter, I mentioned setting up a practice session with Hoskins in 1993 wherein I made several suggestions to improve his game. Two weeks later, he notched his first championship at Grand Prairie, Texas. Like Monacelli, Hoskins extended his nonbowling arm forward with his palms upward and unleashed one of the most potent strike balls in the game.

Bob Learn Jr. and Ryan Shafer also use the shifting and realigning approach. Learn has bowled more than 60 sanctioned 300 games, and he gained worldwide fame on national television in 1996 in Erie, Pennsylvania, by averaging 282 over four games, including one 300 game. Even so, Learn's success has been sporadic; he has recorded only three other victories over an 18-year professional career.

Ryan Shafer joined the PBA Tour in 1986 and was voted Rookie of the Year in 1987. Although he had failed to win in his early years on the Tour, he managed to eke out a living while gaining valuable experience. Shafer had a record of earning the most money of any bowler without a title.

He finally broke through with two victories in 2000 and has established himself as one of the top players on the PBA Tour.

In view of these players' relatively limited success, it's safe to assume that the conventional approach of walking toward your target has a decided advantage over a leftward approach that requires a subsequent shift in direction, opening of the hips and shoulders, and realignment to the intended target. Indeed, with all due credit to Weber, Himmler, Hoskins, Learn, and Shafer, several other power players have not fared as well.

Bob Spaulding, whose booming strike ball was among the most potent on tour, proved that power alone does not ensure success in the PBA. He struggled on drier conditions, and his erratic shots on anything less than a full rack branded him as one of the poorest spare shooters on the Tour. Spaulding recorded his only title at Grand Prairie, Texas, in 1995, the same year in which Mike Aulby defeated him in the Brunswick Tournament of Champions. Spaulding won US$109,927 in 1995, but his inability to temper his devastating strike ball and his woeful spare game forced his retirement from the PBA Tour.

Like Spaulding, Kelly Coffman was a prime example of wasted power. Regarded as possessing the most powerful ball on tour, Coffman delighted in applying maximum revolutions on the ball to warrant his reputation. Absorbed by his obsession with potency and oblivious to the results, he seemingly derived greater satisfaction from ripping racks on light hits than from adjusting his game for solid pocket shots. Coffman and Spaulding were both perennial members of the Jowdy All-Miss Team (Miserable In Spare Situations), which was featured in an annual column listing five or six of the poorest spare shooters on the professional tour.

Coffman's 12 years on the PBA Tour were the greatest misuse of raw talent I have ever witnessed. He was strong, healthy, and extremely pleasant. His strike ball was second to none. To my knowledge, he never abused his body with drugs, tobacco, or alcohol. He had all the tools to be a winner. He could have, and should have, been a real star. I sincerely believed he had the makings of a winner on the professional circuit, and, during a PBA tournament in California, I arranged a practice session and made several recommendations to diversify his game. Although the practice session provided instant improvement, he reverted to his normal method of execution in tournament play. He retired from the Tour less than a year later with nary a title to his credit.

Throughout the country, youngsters are being reared on soft conditions that favor wide-hooking balls. Thousands of 300 games and 800 series are recorded yearly, and players who specialize in opening up the lanes have rung up the majority of these honors. However, because of the overall practice of lane blocking to increase scores, these high marks have become insignificant. The true ability of a bowler is manifested on honest lane conditions—those offered by PBA maintenance crews and organized sport leagues in bowling centers across the nation.

Choosing Your Equipment

Serious bowlers pursue all avenues to remain competitive, and this includes staying abreast of new developments in equipment. Indeed, during the past 20 years, the bowling game has undergone a technological phase. Bowling ball covers have been designed to improve strike percentage; bowling shoes have been devised to improve the sliding process; and numerous wrist, arm, and finger supports have been created—some to prevent pain and injury, others to provide greater stability in the release. These innovations have affected the game profoundly.

Tailor the Ball to Your Game

Bowling balls have evolved from the original wood to rubber, and then on to polyester, urethane, reactive urethane, and proactive urethane materials. From the 1920s to the late 1950s, bowling balls were made of rubber and were limited in scope but unlimited in longevity. The average bowler used *one* ball for more than an entire league season—sometimes up to five years or even longer. Elite bowlers, particularly staff members of bowling ball companies and players of nationally sponsored teams, encountered little difficulty in acquiring new equipment. In the United States, the average cost of bowling balls in the 1940s was less than $18; in the late 1950s, it was about $25. This was the golden age of the game—an era that emphasized league play and team bowling.

Today, a top-caliber bowler may be content to carry four to seven balls in his or her arsenal: perhaps two for oily lanes, two for medium lanes, two for dry lanes, and one hard-surfaced ball (preferably polyester) for spares. To be competitive in the 21st century, however, a bowler must have a complete arsenal, including balls that hook at different lengths down the lane to maximize scoring. This variety can be achieved only through bringing a range of balls that feature differing cores and shells.

High-average bowlers own at least 4 and as many as 30 balls. You can make each ball react in a certain way by altering the shell, core, and method of drilling. Some balls will go long and flip hard on the back end. Others will go long with a gradual arc on the back end. Some are designed to hook early with a strong back end, and others hook early with a smooth reaction on the back end. Experience will tell you which ball to use on which lane condition for maximum striking power. (See chapter 2 for more on reading lane conditions.)

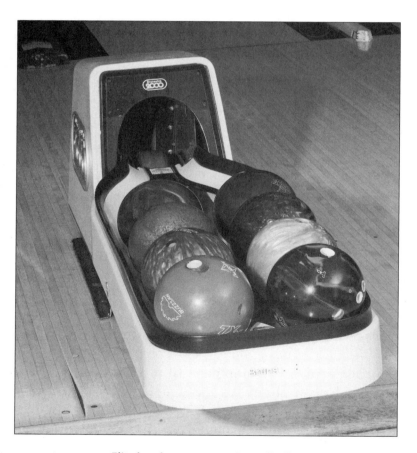

Elite bowlers carry a variety of balls.

The ball's path is affected by several variables. The radius of gyration (RG) determines how soon a ball hooks. RG is a measurement of the ball's moment of inertia—its resistance to revving up. The differential RG determines how much a ball can flare to create more friction with the lane.

Friction on the lane is also affected by the ball's shell material. Polyester shells hook very little and are primarily used to pick up single-pin spares. Urethane shells create a medium amount of hook with a smooth arcing motion. A reactive shell causes the ball to slide in the oil and hook sharply on the dry back end of the lane. Shells that contain particles create friction in the oiled area of the lane for more hook overall, especially in the front of the lane. Thus, serious bowlers need an assortment of balls to compete on all lane conditions they will encounter.

With top-of-the-line balls costing around US$200, it can be expensive to keep an array of options. However, many bowlers feel that the more balls they have to choose from, the less they will have to adjust their physical technique to create the shots they want. On the other hand, while a wide range of bowling balls affords many options for scoring, some bowlers become flustered and confused with too many balls at their disposal. As a result, some top players on the PBA Tour carry fewer bowling balls and prefer to overcome difficult conditions by changing speed and hand position.

Customizing the Right Fit

The key is to select a ball that fits your hand and your game. Take these factors into consideration when fitting a bowler with a functional grip:

✗ Span—the distance between the holes used for the purpose of grip

✗ Pitch—the angle at which the hole is drilled into the bowling ball

✗ Hole size and shape—the internal measurements and shape of the drilled inserts in the bowling ball

Two basic types of grip exist:

1. Conventional grip (figure 11.1a). The fingers are inserted to the second joint with the thumb seated in properly. When the fingers are inserted into the holes, each finger forms a 90-degree angle. The conventional grip makes it easier to roll a straight ball but more difficult to impart rotation. This grip is popular with recreational bowlers.

2. Fingertip grip (figure 11.1b). In this grip, the fingers are inserted only to the first joint. The thumb is seated in properly, with the knuckle

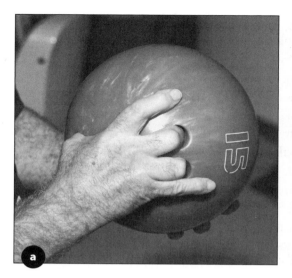

Figure 11.1   Basic grips: *(a)* conventional grip; *(b)* fingertip grip.

slightly raised from the ball. This grip should allow the first joint to stay in contact with the leading edge of the finger hole so that the fingers form a 90-degree angle into the hole. This drilling method is used by highly skilled bowlers, since fingertip grips make it easier to create rotation on the ball.

Ball-drilling experts consider the following factors when fitting a ball to a bowler:

✗ The length of the bowling hand determines the distance between the holes.

✗ Hand, wrist, and elbow strength are factors in determining the proper weight of a bowling ball. One must also take into account any relevant health conditions, such as carpal tunnel syndrome, arthritis, and tendinitis.

✗ The flexibility of the hand and fingers plays a major role in determining pitch. As you grow older, flexibility decreases. Bowlers who work principally with their hands will experience differing degrees of flexibility.

✗ Skin texture plays a role in diminishing pitch. Some hands are smooth and dry; others are rough and moist. Those with smooth and dry hands benefit from less reverse pitch or more forward pitch. Conversely, those with moist skin require more reverse pitch.

I suggest regular visits to a certified bowling technician at any bowling pro shop displaying the IBPSIA (International Bowling Pro Shop and Instructors Association) logo. Certified bowling technicians can fit you properly.

Changes in hands and fingers can occur quickly, and ignoring proper grip adjustments may cause physical problems and adversely affect your bowling. According to internationally renowned ball-drilling expert and former IBPSIA president Jerry Francomano, "No matter how good you are, you can't outbowl a bad fit."

Hole size is another important factor. Although a competent driller will concede on the size of the hole somewhat in order to satisfy the bowler, rarely will he or she relent on span or pitch. Most skilled players prefer a tighter hole. Most bowlers use tape to adjust hole sizes to get the perfect feel, particularly in the thumbhole. Less skilled players tend to use larger thumbholes, then apply and adjust tape to a smaller size. When their level of proficiency increases, they drill new balls.

Although this chapter includes a discussion of basic drilling patterns (see sidebar), I have omitted treatment of all drilling *techniques* because the ever-changing technology of modern ball construction would render my suggestions ineffectual. Today's refined bowling balls—forged of changing materials and built with sophisticated, strategically placed weight blocks—are packaged with drilling instructions. Pro shop operators stay abreast of all new innovations by attending drilling seminars sponsored by bowling ball manufacturers. I urge you to choose an accredited, competent expert and rely on his or her judgment. I recommend the experienced services of any certified member of IBPSIA.

Axis weight refers to a drilling pattern designed to produce little or no track flare in order to get the ball into an early roll with little back-end reaction. The pin is located on or near the bowler's PAP. The core is positioned along the initial spin axis—the minimum-radius-of-gyration (RG) axis—and since this is a stable core position, the ball continues to rotate around it, thus creating no track flare and reducing back-end reaction. Since the ball rotates about the low-RG axis, it is easier for the bowler to rotate it off of his or her hand.

Leverage drilling is a pattern that produces maximum track flare. The pin and center of gravity (CG) are located 3 3/8 inches (8.6 centimeters) from the bowler's PAP, placing the core at a 45-degree angle to the axis line—an unstable position for a dynamic core. The core moves away from this location, causing track flare, which increases the friction between the ball and the lane, thus getting the ball into an early roll. Depending

Basic Drilling Patterns

Drilling experts customize drill patterns by starting with the bowler's positive axis point (PAP), which is the location on the ball about which the ball initially rotates. The expert finds the PAP by determining the point on the ball that is equidistant from the initial ball track—that is, before the ball flares. This refers to the first oil ring on the ball and is the one closest to the thumbhole. For a three-quarter roller (with the ball track just outside of the fingers and thumb), the PAP is approximately 5 inches (13 centimeters) from the center of the grip along the midline and about a half-inch (1.3 centimeters) up along the vertical axis line (see figure 11.2). To verify this track, you can place a piece of tape on the ball at this location and have a friend observe your bowling. When the ball first comes off your hand and contacts the lane, the tape should spin in place without moving around the ball—that is, if it is on the PAP, it should appear stationary. The PAP for a left-handed bowler is on the left side of the grip; therefore, a ball is drilled in the opposite manner for a left-handed bowler.

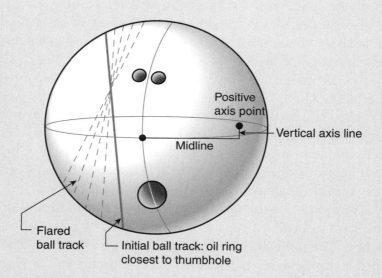

Figure 11.2 The positive axis point (PAP) for a right-handed bowler. A left-handed bowler would have the PAP on the left side of the grip, and the ball track would be on the right side. Therefore, drilling patterns for a left-hander are reversed.

Drilling patterns are techniques used to change the initial position of the core in the ball to alter both its flare potential and the distance it travels down the lane before it starts to hook. Generally, more flare is associated with more hook because it increases the friction by keeping a dry area of the ball, instead of an oily area, in contact with the lane. Figure 11.3 shows how flare potential and ball reaction change with different pin positions.

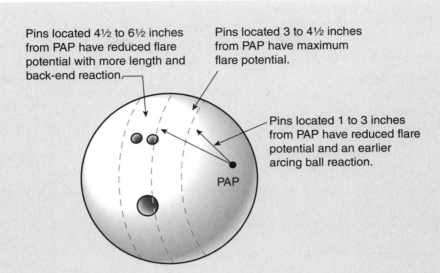

Pins located 4½ to 6½ inches from PAP have reduced flare potential with more length and back-end reaction.

Pins located 3 to 4½ inches from PAP have maximum flare potential.

Pins located 1 to 3 inches from PAP have reduced flare potential and an earlier arcing ball reaction.

PAP

Figure 11.3   Flare potential and ball reaction of different pin positions.

The pin position is important because it is the end of the core. By locating the pin at different distances from the PAP, we can create different motions in the same ball. The center of gravity (CG) is the heaviest point on the ball. Moving it to different locations has the same effect as moving the pin, but it has less impact on the pins.

For example, if a ball is drilled with the pin at 3 inches (7.6 centimeters) and the CG is at 1 inch (2.5 centimeters), it will have maximum flare from the pin position. But, it will start hooking earlier with an arcing breakpoint because of the CG position. Here are the expected results and preferred conditions for various drilling patterns.

Early Hook With Flip Drilling

Pin-to-PAP distance
3 3/8 to 4 inches (8.6 to 10.2 centimeters)
CG-to-PAP distance
3 3/8 to 4 inches

Result: Creates track flare to give maximum friction between ball and lane; early breakpoint and sharp turn.

Preferred lane condition: Best for oily lane conditions, with and without carry-down.

Drawbacks: Can use up friction early, resulting in early rollout; bowlers with an early-roll style (12–15) may have their breakpoint too early.

(continued)

Early Roll With Arc Drilling

Pin-to-PAP distance
3 3/8 inches (8.6 centimeters)
CG-to-PAP distance
0 to 2 inches (5.1 centimeters)

Result: Arcing ball path; starts hooking in oil, which reduces the flipping motion at the breakpoint. This drilling requires a dry back end to allow the ball to finish.

Preferred lane condition: Best for oily heads with some dry boards (for example, down the lane or outside).

Drawback: Carry-down on the back ends reduces hitting power.

Extended Length With Strong Arc Finish

Pin-to-PAP distance
5 to 6 1/2 inches (12.7 to 16.5 centimeters)
CG-to-PAP distance
3 3/8 to 4 inches (8.6 to 10.2 centimeters)

Result: Minimum track flare to reduce friction and get the ball farther down the lane to create the latest breakpoint.

Preferred lane conditions: Best for medium to dry lane and dry back end; also performs well on second shift condition when the heads have dried up.

Drawback: May tend to go too long and not flip enough on carry-down.

Caution: A pin shift of more than 6 3/4 inches causes the track to flare in the wrong direction (toward the thumbhole instead of away). Therefore, use caution when drilling the 6- and 6 1/2-inch pin shift to ensure that the pin-to-PAP distance is correct.

Label Drilling

Pin-to-PAP distance
4 to 5 inches (10.2 to 12.7 centimeters)
CG-to-PAP distance
near grip

Results: Reduces flip on the back end, creating a strong, arcing back end and an average distance to the breakpoint.

Preferred lane condition: Fresh lane condition with oily heads and dry to medium back ends; does not overreact on back end.

Drawback: Loses hitting power as the shot moves in deep because it does not have a strong back-end flip.

The information on drilling patterns was provided by Jerry Francomano and is used with his permission.

on the bowler's style, the added friction can increase the sharpness of the turn at the breakpoint, especially for low-RPM bowlers. For higher-RPM bowlers, however, the added friction can cause the ball to slow down too much in the oil; the ball's energy is expended in the oil, where the ball cannot hook very easily, thus reducing the turn at the breakpoint.

Determining the Best Ball Weight

The primary factors in selecting the right ball are your comfort in using the ball and the scoring ability of the ball. Most PBA bowlers use 16-pound (7.3-kilogram) balls, but many of them have dropped to 15-pound (6.8-kilogram) balls to minimize the effects of today's powerful missiles. Believe it or not, some players have even dropped to 14-pound (6.4-kilogram) balls. However, a 14-pound ball is more inclined to deflect off the head pin and fail to carry through the pocket; therefore, it is not recommended for those who can handle a heavier weight. At any rate, throw whatever weight feels comfortable, as long as the carrying percentage isn't seriously impaired.

There are no restrictions on minimum weight for bowling balls. In fact, most bowling ball companies make balls ranging from 6 to 16 pounds (2.7 to 7.3 kilograms). Balls in the range of 6 to 11 pounds (5 kilograms) are designed for children who gradually increase the weight as they grow older. Although most women in the professional ranks use 15-pound (6.8-kilogram) or 16-pound balls, those in the 12- to 14-pound (5.4- to 6.4-kilogram) range are the normal choice for women who engage in bowling on the recreational level.

The maximum weight for a bowling ball is 16 pounds (7.3 kilograms), but 16-pound balls are normally manufactured with a gross weight of approximately 16 pounds 2 ounces to compensate for the 2 or 3 ounces removed during the drilling process. Two of the most noted professionals, Mike Aulby and Amleto Monacelli, use 15-pound (6.8-kilogram) balls instead of 16-pounders in order to minimize the hard-hitting effects. This philosophy was credited to ABC Hall of Famer Dave Davis, who used 14-pound (6.4-kilogram) balls during the latter portion of his career. Many knowledgeable observers subscribe to this theory, particularly with the advent of modern, hard-driving, urethane balls. Nonetheless, the majority of players on the PBA Tour continue to bowl with 16-pound balls.

Altering Ball Surfaces With Sandpaper

Bowlers can use sandpaper to alter bowling balls slightly in order to meet the requirements for assorted lane conditions. Although ABC regulations prohibit the practice of forming a track in the ball with a foreign substance, it is permissible to sand the entire surface of the ball. If properly applied, sandpaper can profoundly affect ball reaction. Now, however, manufacturers are producing bowling balls with tremendous tracking surfaces, and many PBA players find the use of sandpaper increasingly unnecessary.

Those who do use it can find assorted grades or grits of sandpaper, and each produces a different reaction from the ball. One must use caution in applying sandpaper, since incorrect application may prevent restoration of the ball to its original state. The use of any grade of sandpaper under 400 grit greatly enhances the biting effect of the ball on the lanes. Bowlers who seek additional traction by applying grittier sandpaper run the risk of early hook and may experience the consequences of the rollout factor on dry back ends. Although rollout can be overcome through the use of excessive speed, this strategy can, in many situations, profoundly hamper a bowler's rhythm and timing and thus be counterproductive.

Sandpaper can also be used to apply a high-polish finish to a ball. A 600-grit paper is used for a medium to smooth finish, whereas grits in the 1,000 to 2,000 range are used for a high polish. On the other hand, Scotch-Brite has become the most widely used product for removing the glaze on new balls. In fact, ingenious bowlers have mastered the art of Scotch-Briting the track in a ball to preserve the skidding effect in the early part of the lane yet maintain an advantage for traction in the hooking stage of the lane.

Understanding Advancements in Ball Material

The original bowling balls were made of wood; wooden balls are no longer used, but they are on display at the International Bowling Museum and Hall of Fame in St. Louis. Rubber balls were originally made of pure rubber, but when the United States became involved in World War II in the early 1940s, rubber became an important commodity for military use, and synthetic rubber became the alternative for civilian use. At that time, the most noted manufacturers of rubber balls in the United States were Ace, Brunswick, Ebonite, and Manhattan. Black was the primary color used by male bowlers, but other colors in mottled designs were available, particularly for women and children.

During the late 1950s, polyester balls were introduced. They featured sparkling colors and, more important, displayed greater traction on the lanes—an advantage that offered higher scoring potential.

Polyester Balls

Before proceeding any further, I feel compelled to define *polyester*. All too often, bowlers use the word *plastic* to refer to polyester balls. This has, in fact, been the most misused word in the bowling lexicon. The word *plastic* denotes a human-made concoction of various unnatural resins. The correct term for bowling balls is *polyester*. In the late 1950s, polyester balls were produced and widely marketed by Brunswick and Columbia 300, and soon they were also being manufactured by AMF, Ebonite, and Manhattan. Polyester balls eventually replaced rubber balls, since they featured greater hooking traction and came in a variety of colors. The top price for multicolored polyester balls was US$25 each.

In the early 1970s, Don McCune devised a method for softening the shell of a bowling ball through the application of highly flammable chemical solutions which combined methyl ethyl ketone and toluene. The softened outer shell created greater tracking action on the lanes, and this newfound magic transformed McCune from journeyman status to Bowler of the Year in 1973. McCune won five titles, became the leading money winner for the year, and gained recognition as the originator of the *soaker*, the popular term for balls soaked in a bucket of chemicals. Not long after, because of the volatility of these chemicals, the PBA was compelled to outlaw this practice.

Nonetheless, since softer ball surfaces provided desirable traction on the lanes, Columbia 300 introduced the Sur D bowling ball in 1974. It was a soft ball that registered less than 68 on the Shur-D Durometer (a device used to measure the surface hardness of a bowling ball.) The Sur D ball provided the greatest hooking traction ever seen at that time; in fact, it dominated the 1974 ABC Masters tournament as no other ball in history ever had. No fewer than 15 of the top 16 finalists used the Sur D ball. Its soft surface was far more susceptible to scratches and gouges and often showed indentations when placed on a ball ring in warmer weather, but bowlers, basking in the glory of newfound powers, simply ignored the marring and purchased new balls.

The Sur D ball became so revolutionary that the American Bowling Congress instituted a regulation rendering illegal all balls that registered less than 72 degrees on the hardness scale. The Professional Bowlers Association went further by raising the hardness standard to 75. The new rules forced manufacturers to seek materials that met the standards yet provided bowlers with equipment that enhanced ball performance on the lanes. A short time later, Columbia 300 produced the Yellow Dot, a polyester ball that met the 75-degree hardness rule yet provided greater traction than any other ball on the market. The Yellow Dot dominated the professional tour for three or four years.

In 1974, John Fabovich, a ball designer, introduced the first bowling ball with a two-piece weight block in polyester material. It was the birth of Faball and, though the two-piece weight block had some redeeming qualities, it made little or no impact on the industry—that is, at that time. Fabovich's design was intended to create excess power in bowling balls. Weight blocks were placed in various positions within the ball that would enhance extra drive in the ball's path to the pocket. As we shall see, Fabovich's innovation would make a considerable impact on the bowling ball industry down the line.

In 1976, a rubber ball with incredible traction characteristics made its mark on the PBA Tour. Designed by Louis Trier, a 48-year-old Brunswick engineer, it was appropriately named the Brunswick LT-48. Within a year, Brunswick's superstar, Johnny Petraglia, endorsed the ball, and it became the Johnny Petraglia LT-48. The LT-48 replaced the Yellow Dot as the most popular ball on the PBA Tour and had a successful run through the 1970s and early 1980s.

Urethane Balls

In the early 1980s, AMF introduced the Angle, the first urethane ball approved by the American Bowling Congress. Although the price (US$89) seemed prohibitive, the ball took the game by storm and practically eliminated other high-performance balls. The newly discovered urethane material exhibited greater traction on the lanes than any other. Skeptics expressed doubts about bowling balls that could retail for $89, but price did not stem the tide of record-setting sales for the Angle. Inevitably, other manufacturers followed suit.

In the early 1980s, John Fabovich sold Faball to two St. Louis bowlers, John Wonders and Earl Widman, who began production of two-piece weight-block balls with urethane materials. Faball realized instant success with a catchy brand name—the Hammer—which performed fairly well on the PBA Tour in its original black color. A short time later, Faball introduced the Blue Hammer, which became not only the rage of the PBA Tour but also the choice of elite bowlers all over the country until around 1989.

In the meantime, Storm bowling balls began to make a big splash on the bowling scene with an assortment of high-performance balls. The

Utah-based company made great inroads among the world's elite bowlers and rode its wave of popularity for a number of years before losing its hold on the high-performance market to the Brunswick Corporation and Ebonite International.

Around 2004, Ebonite International purchased Faball from John Wonders and reestablished Hammer's popularity. Later, in 2007, Ebonite acquired Columbia 300, which included the Columbia, Track, and Dyno-thane lines of bowling balls.

Reactive urethane balls In late 1989, a California native, Steve Cooper, launched the Excalibur, a ball that provided the greatest tracking action of anything ever produced. This was the first ball featuring a reactive coverstock, and the word *reactive* crept into bowling jargon. It describes the hooking action of the ball, which derives from the greater friction the ball creates on the lane. Unsurprisingly, within a year, every manufacturer jumped on the reactive ball bandwagon.

Proactive urethane balls In the late 1990s, Brunswick introduced its Proactive ball constructed of urethane resins containing gritty particles. The gritty contents enabled the ball to literally claw into the lanes and create a greater hooking effect. Naturally, all other manufacturers followed Brunswick's lead, and *proactive* became another word in the bowling vernacular.

Although new innovations in bowling ball materials created greater traction on the lanes and provided bowlers with a clear advantage for strike percentage, the new materials caused trouble for lane maintenance crews worldwide. The greater oil absorption of urethane balls, caused by their porosity, literally ate up lane dressings. Porosity refers to the soft-ness or the absorbency of a given material and is the determining factor for coefficient of friction. The softer or more abrasive the shell of the ball, the less the skid factor, and thus the greater advantage of traction and the increased chance of higher scoring.

Although most of the recently skyrocketing scores result from doc-tored lane conditions, the American Bowling Congress and the Women's International Bowling Congress took further steps to control the scoring madness by sanctioning the revision of two important specifications for all bowling balls. In early 2001, the equipment specification committees of both the ABC and the WIBC approved the tightening of the upper-average specifications of the friction coefficient of bowling balls (from 0.39 to 0.32). The revision applies to any new ball and to the remanufacture of any previously approved ball. Any bowling ball currently approved will remain on the approved ball list. These figures apply solely to bowling ball manufacturers. The new specifications also place a limit on the porosity factor allowed in all future manufacturing and therefore will somewhat limit hooking ability.

Unbelievable as it may seem, modern bowling balls for elite players are priced in the range of US$210 to US$225. New balls are being introduced at a monthly rate, each featuring a variety of claims of supremacy. There is, however, no built-in magic in any ball. Proper execution inevitably overcomes any coverstock, weight block, pin placement, or other innovation.

Select the Right Shoe

From the 1930s to the 1950s, a period when bowling balls lasted many seasons, bowling shoes lasted perhaps 10 years, depending on the amount of use. Like most modern bowling shoes, they had a leather sole for slid-

Pro players recognize the importance of having shoes that can handle a variety of approach conditions.

ing and a rubber sole for braking. In the 1930s, the shoe of choice for top bowlers was the Jimmy Smith brand; it was constructed of high-quality leather and sold for less than US$10.

Since then, bowling shoes have undergone tremendous changes, as manufacturers have continually responded to the desire for shoes that work on varying lane conditions and suit bowlers with different styles. During the 1940s and 1950s, Hyde bowling shoes were the choice of better bowlers. There was one exception, however: Lind custom-made shoes. The sliding capacity of Lind shoes, along with their unique red kidskin material, revolutionized the game. Top-rated players chose Lind shoes that had to be special-ordered and necessitated premeasurements. Today, Lind shoes are displayed in pro shops all over the United States.

When it comes to footwear, you have a choice between renting and buying. Rental shoes are a staple in bowling centers for the convenience of occasional recreational bowlers. But rental shoes have two sliding soles, rather than one sole for sliding and one for braking, which means that they are not conducive to good bowling. Rental shoes merely fill the need for those who are not serious about the game. Your best bet is to invest in a good pair of shoes that matches your bowling style and can handle a variety of approach conditions. For example, if you use a longer slide on the approach, get shoes with a sliding sole. If you use more of a braking style, gets shoes with soles that stop the fastest. Strokers often opt for a softer sliding sole, whereas power players prefer a braking sole. Choose shoes with the sole and heel that best fit your style of play.

Atmospheric conditions can seriously affect approaches. Weather influences lane patterns and also affects approaches. Slippery approaches hamper braking, whereas other approaches become tacky and prevent a smooth slide; as a result, professional bowlers rely as much on bowling shoes as on bowling balls—or maybe even more.

Bowling shoes are so much better today because they give you so many variations. These days, you bowl on lighter wood or synthetic approaches, and they slide differently. Then you have the humidity factor, high or low, which also affects sliding conditions. Bowling is a sport like any other sport. If you want to play it well, you have to go out and buy the very best equipment for your game. Spending $30 [US] on a pair of shoes is not going to help your game.

Johnny Petraglia
PBA Hall of Famer and Senior Tour member

The Lind Shoe Story

The Lind shoe story reads like a Horatio Alger novel. In 1919, Leslie Lind and his father, Erick, ran a small shop in St. Paul, Minnesota, that made shoes for wealthy railroad and lumber executives, as well as ice skates and dancing slippers.

One day in 1936, a man from Hamm's Brewery came to the shop. The gentleman was a member of the Hamm's bowling team and wanted to know whether the Linds had anything that would slide. Lind had a piece of buckskin and agreed to attach a piece of this material to the sole of the bowling shoe.

The next day, the man returned with the rest of the team to outfit them all. Lind said he could make a shoe that would serve the sport better than what was currently available and offered to make shoes for the team. The team liked the idea but wanted something that would really stand out. Lind decided to try the red kidskin he had used in designing shoes for a Ukrainian dance troupe.

The Hamm's team loved them and used them in a match against the Stroh's Beer team in Detroit. The Stroh's team called Lind shortly after the match to request the same shoes, and, war years notwithstanding, they purchased the new red kidskins annually thereafter.

In 1941, Lind joined the armed services and closed the shop. After returning from the war, he began making specialized shoes for the Veterans Administration. He found the work rewarding because without these shoes many of the disabled veterans would not have been able to walk. However, knowing the VA business had its limitations and would soon make their own shoes, he continued to make a few bowling shoes. As demand grew, bowlers had to wait weeks, even months, to receive the made-to-fit shoes that sold for US$45 to US$60, a rather exorbitant cost at that time.

In 1968, Leslie Lind's son, Jeff, joined the firm. During his early years with the company, Jeff answered the phone and mail and had the opportunity to speak with many bowlers. He learned a great deal about the bowling business and thought changes in business policy were necessary. Orders were piling up; they were 18 months behind, and something had to be done. In 1970, Lind Shoe Company moved to Stillwater, Minnesota, just east of St. Paul. They occupied an old abandoned shoe factory and invested in new equipment, and things started to look good—so good, in fact, that they were opening the mail in the morning and making the shoes that afternoon.

In 1976, Lind wrote to his 10 best customers (pro shops) and offered them shoes in stock sizes, white, D width only, with a minimum order of 12 pairs. Today, Lind features shoes in every size and color, as well as interchangeable soles and heels—all designed to meet an individual bowler's needs.

Today's high-performance bowling shoes feature inserts and interchangeable heels and soles designed to alter sliding and braking patterns in order to meet any approach condition. Such features can be beneficial but are not an absolute *must* for all bowlers who take the game seriously. The principal objective is to make certain that the sliding sole is constructed of smooth leather and the opposite sole of soft rubber. Although the majority of bowlers are content with conventional heels, a raised or lowered heel can also regulate sliding patterns. A raised heel lessens the slide; a lowered heel increases it. The majority of PBA and high-level amateur bowlers place extreme emphasis on the sliding soles of their shoes, and they include a wire brush among their accessories for maintaining clean sliding soles and avoiding any mishaps in sliding patterns.

> In the old days, we worried about the sliding foot, but now we know that we must also have the best shoe possible on the pushaway foot. With these new combinations, you can create sticky soles on the nonsliding foot, which can give you good leverage at the foul line.
>
> *Earl Anthony*
> *PBA and ABC Hall of Famer*

Dexter began making bowling shoes in 1961 and is now one of America's largest shoe manufacturers. The company entered the market for high-performance bowling shoes in 1988 by introducing the SST shoe line and hired David Ozio as its PBA representative. Ozio and other professionals recommended various designs and styles that made it possible to alter the power pivot sole for the nonsliding shoe. Dexter offered not only interchangeable soles but also interchangeable heels featuring assorted attachable and removable Velcro inserts designed to change sliding and braking patterns in 16 combinations. In 2005, during a major downsizing of upper-echelon personnel, Dexter broke ties with David Ozio.

In 2004, Etonic made a major impact in the bowling shoe market. The company began slowly by catering to lower-average bowlers, then gained prominence among elite bowlers. Moreover, they hired David Ozio, who was fresh off his parting of the ways with Dexter.

> I don't think the league bowlers—even the good ones—realize how important the bowling shoe is to their game. If a bowler starts leaving a weak 10 or if his or her bowling ball is hitting flat, they may not be getting good leverage, and it's time to try a new sole or inserts.
>
> *John Handegard*
> *14-time senior titlist; senior Player of the Year in 1991, 1995, 1996*

Although Lind, Dexter, and Etonic have revolutionized bowling shoes with their interchangeable soles, heels, and inserts, this innovative concept must be credited to Riedell Shoes of Red Wing, Minnesota. Riedell specialized in the production of ice skates and had numerous outlets, particularly for hockey skates. In the early 1950s, Paul Riedell received a call from Max Lubin, proprietor of a sporting goods store in Massachusetts. Lubin specialized in hockey and bowling equipment. Riedell recommended a bowling shoe, called the Joe McCord, with removable ovals in the center of the sole. For whatever reason, however, the Riedell concept did not have the impact on bowlers of that era that today's sophisticated bowling shoes do.

Pick the Best Accessories

Bowlers can make use of various accessories—bags, hand and wrist supports, tapes, grips, inserts, towels, and skin treatments—to enhance their game. Some bowlers use no special equipment at all, but many prefer some kind of support. Female bowlers use wrist and grip supports more often than their male counterparts do.

Bowling Bags

Bowling bags come in all sizes and shapes. Recreational bowlers can purchase one-ball bags that provide space for one pair of shoes. They are available at pro shops as well as sporting goods and department stores; two-ball bags are also available at department stores.

Bowling bags have undergone considerable change over the past 20 years. During the 1970s and 1980s, Triangle and Colonial bags were the popular choices among elite bowlers. Each featured metal frames to secure balls, ample space below for storing shoes, and additional space for accessories.

In the late 1980s, ball manufacturers commissioned companies in Korea and Taiwan to produce the most sophisticated bowling bags imaginable. Bags were built to hold two, three, and four balls, with ample space provided as well for shoes and accessories. Effectively, these bags functioned as luggage, complete with wheels. They also became more costly. Professionals and top amateurs carry three or more luggage-type bags to store their equipment. PBA players are restricted to eight balls at a time in the locker area, which is an excessive amount considering the limited space allotted in the players' area at most bowling centers. Along with balls, professional bowlers also carry repair items and tape or glue for inserts.

Hand and Wrist Supports

The market has been flooded with various devices for the arm, elbow, forearm, wrist, and finger; all are designed or marketed to aid in shot execution. They are more noticeable among professional female bowlers. For example, Carolyn Dorin-Ballard and Wendy Macpherson wear wrist supports.

It is interesting to note that superstars Chris Barnes, Parker Bohn III, Norm Duke, Amleto Monacelli, and Walter Ray Williams shun performance-enhancing gadgets. Nonetheless, Jason Couch, Tim Criss, and Ryan Shafer sport either wrist, hand, or arm supports to help them execute high-quality shots.

One of the more unusual accessories is a glove worn by Pete Weber. Its construction is similar to that of a golfer's glove—that is, it covers the

Many professional female bowlers, such as Clara Guerrero, wear wrist supports to aid in their release.

hand. Weber, however, uses his glove solely as a protection for his fingers; it has no effect whatsoever on his game.

Although some hand and wrist supports appear to be cumbersome and uncomfortable, they have proven beneficial to many bowlers, particularly some female bowlers. Many wrist supports are devised to prevent the breaking back of the wrist, thereby ensuring a firmer release. Nevertheless, some of the greatest releases among top-rated bowlers feature a broken-back wrist with a rapid forward acceleration (as discussed in detail in chapter 6).

Several years ago, the splint (a forearm support) was introduced to the bowling world. Consisting of thin straps worn around the area between the wrist and elbow, the splint was designed as preventive maintenance for tendons in the forearm. This innovation was very helpful for six-time title winner Roger Bowker, who uses an unusual stance in which he extends the ball with his right arm rested against his hip—a position that places extreme strain on the forearm. After sustaining strained tendons in his forearm, Bowker began using the splint. He derived great satisfaction from this device and, though he no longer wears it, the splint prolonged his career.

Hand, wrist, and arm accessories are a matter of preference. In many cases, they have become a mental comfort, and on the professional level they serve as a source of income for players who endorse them. Whether they enhance a player's performance, however, may be debatable. For example, years ago, a major glove manufacturer formed an advisory staff, which hired a group of top-rated stars on a monthly retainer fee. The principal feature of this glove was a padded palm that placed the ball firmly in the hand. Nevertheless, one of the top players on the star-studded staff removed the palm pad and simply wore the glove. It merely covered his hand and fingers and had absolutely no effect on his release. When asked if the gadget helped him, he simply replied without hesitation, "Yeah, about $100 [US] a month."

Tape

Thumbs and fingers are prone to shrinking or swelling, either of which can cause difficulty in gripping or releasing the ball. Tape has become the great adjuster, providing a quick fix for fitting a favorite ball. Tape comes in several textures; plastic and adhesive are the most commonly used, and each can be of great value. Plastic tape, with its slicker composition, promotes instant exiting of either fingers or thumb and acts as a deterrent to hanging in the ball. Adhesive tape, similar to medical tape, is courser; it affords better grip than plastic tape does and can delay the exiting of the thumb or fingers. It is applied on the front area of the thumb to achieve two purposes:

1. It prevents the bowler from squeezing the ball out of fear of dropping it in the backswing, thus allowing the bowler to exercise a relaxed swing.

2. It provides a firmer grip with the thumb, which simplifies the shifting of the ball weight from the thumb to the fingers at the release point. Although this might seem to conflict with the slower-releasing tendency of adhesive tape, it must be noted that the thumb has arrived at the release point in a flat plane, and the transferring of the weight from the thumb to the fingers is simplified through the freeing of the thumb grasp.

I firmly advocate the natural, rapid exit of the thumb, particularly for bowlers with flexible hands. Consequently, I do not recommend adhesive tape on the back part of the thumb. I would suggest plastic tape for the back of the thumb because it forms a slicker surface and permits the thumb to exit unimpeded.

Grips and Inserts

Many professional and top amateur bowlers place as much emphasis on thumb and finger inserts as they do on drilling configurations. Unbeknownst to many contemporary players, inserts were in vogue as far back as the 1940s, particularly among bowlers accustomed to using tape to assure a stronger grip in the ball.

The original inserts were made in various sizes for thumbs and fingers. They were called *ovals*. Unlike modern inserts, they did not necessitate drilling, and they were sold in various sizes. Sometime between the late 1940s and the late 1950s, oval inserts disappeared. Also during this era, Manhattan Rubber Company, a leading manufacturer, formulated a ball with a soft rubber texture just below the surface of the ball. The softer material, approximately one-quarter of an inch (0.6 centimeter) below the outer surface, provided a slip-free grip.

During the late 1930s or early 1940s, Ace Mitchell introduced Shur Hooks, which were shaped like modern tape inserts and made of cork material that was ridged for firmer gripping. Shur Hooks dominated the market and were used by almost every elite bowler. Shur Hooks were still in demand until the early 1970s and, though they gave way to modern inserts, they are still an important item in bowling pro shops.

In the early 1960s, Steve Vesarakis, a Californian, invented the Pro Grip, a solid insert of clear material. In 1961, Don Heimbigner bought the product and moved it to Vancouver, Washington. The company became known as Don's Sports Systems, then as Pro Sports Systems, and the inserts became known as Contour Power Grips. Although the clear material did not catch the fancy of the bowling public, it was in compliance with ABC rules designed to prevent cheaters and hustlers from inserting lead below the surface of the ball, a deceptive ploy that jeopardized the integrity of the game. In 1978, Heimbigner met Ernie Schlegel and appointed him as sales representative on the PBA Tour. Thanks to Schlegel's salesmanship, grips were resurrected, and they have become a major force in the modern bowler's arsenal. The numerous competitors in the grip business include Turbo 2-N-1 and Vise Inserts.

Bowling Towels

Bowling towels have become an essential commodity in a bowler's accessory bag. Bowling balls absorb oil on freshly conditioned lanes, and towels are particularly useful for removing oil tracks. They have also become useful advertising vehicles for bowling ball manufacturers, who design towels with logos clearly visible not only to the crowds in attendance but also those watching via television. Nevertheless, towels have become such a fixation that many bowlers wipe balls when the lanes are practically oil-free. Many accessories serve as mental consolations.

Skin Treatments

Bowlers, particularly those who apply excessive effort in executing shots, often experience sore thumbs. Although most PBA strokers are not as susceptible to thumb and finger problems as are other types of bowlers, they can be affected by the rigors of delivering 16-pound (7.3-kilogram) bowling balls day after day and week after week during qualifying and match-play rounds, not to mention many hours of practice. Crankers are particularly vulnerable to sore thumbs; for example, Mark Roth's bowling thumb is considerably larger than his other thumb because of his vigorous release.

It is safe to assume that the majority of skin treatments are derived from the same sources as the original treatment—collodion, a nitrocellulose solution that dries into a tough, elastic film used to protect wounds. The most popular brand among elite players is Robby's Skin Protector. Other skin treatments are available in pro shops, but they are all essentially collodion-related.

Accessories can play an important role in a bowler's arsenal. Each has its purpose and should be incorporated as needed in a bowler's game. But remember: What is good for one bowler is not necessarily good for everyone. And, regardless, the most important equipment for top performance is a properly fitted bowling ball. Accessories such as bags, wrist and hand supports, tape, sandpaper, and skin treatments can enhance a bowler's game, but the only offensive weapon for knocking down pins is a ball that fits comfortably, comes off the hand cleanly, and is released out into the lane with no difficulty. Simply seek the services of a certified bowling technician at any bowling pro shop bearing the International Bowling Pro Shop and Instructors Association (IBPSIA) label.

Competing at the Next Level

There are four ways to play the sport of bowling: league, open play, tournament, and elite. However, if you want to compete at the highest level, the ultimate challenge in competitive bowling is in the elite classification of Sport Bowling and PBA Experience conditions.

League Bowling

Bowling provides endless social and competitive opportunities. One can enjoy the camaraderie of teammates as well as the opportunity to attain personal goals, such as the first 600 series, then the first 700, and, of course, the first 300 game.

League bowling has been the backbone of the sport since the American Bowling Congress (ABC) was formed in 1895. In leagues, people form teams of two, three, four, or five players who compete on a regular basis for a specific period of time. At the end of the season, champions are crowned, usually at a bowling banquet.

League bowling is a tremendous experience. It's a chance to get away from the pressures of daily life, relax, and have fun with friends and family. Nearly all pro bowlers begin their bowling careers by engaging in league play. Children from 3 years on up are taught the game in Learn to Bowl classes; later, they advance into junior leagues and eventually into adult leagues that feature team play.

A bowling league involves a group of people sharing a common interest: the desire to compete regularly in bowling. Often, it involves competing with co-workers or friends from the same church or club. Leagues can consist of as few as 4 teams or as many as 50. Bowlers can find mixed leagues, senior leagues, men's leagues, women's leagues, and any combination thereof. League play can be scheduled during the morning, afternoon, or evening, and on weekdays or weekends.

Most important, players can find leagues for every ability, thanks to a handicap system. In fact, one of the great features of league bowling involves the various divisions of competition. Top-caliber bowlers usually compete in nonhandicap leagues, generally referred to as classic leagues, but aside from these scratch leagues the proven handicap system gives less-talented players the opportunity to bowl on the same team with top performers in an area.

Five-person team bowling—a form of league bowling—has gradually declined during the past 35 years, due principally to the PBA's tremendous impact on individual competition beginning in the early 1960s. Previously, bowling on a great team was the goal of every aspiring bowler in America, since team bowling offered the excitement of competition at the city, state, and national levels. Team bowling on the national level reigned supreme before the organization of the Professional Bowling Association in the early 1960s. Groups from Chicago, Milwaukee, Detroit, Cleveland, St. Louis, and the New York–New Jersey area fielded teams with star-studded line-ups, many of whom became ABC Hall of Famers. Staunch corporate supporters included the following breweries: Budweiser, Falstaff, Hamm's, Meister Brau, Monarch, Pfeiffer, and Stroh.

Teams made up the strongest leagues in bowling history and annually competed in the Bowling Proprietors Association of America (BPAA) All-Star Championships. However, with the emergence of the PBA, team bowling lost its appeal, and Budweiser superstars such as Ray Bluth, Don Carter, Bill Lillard, and Dick Weber—as well as Falstaff members Glen Allison, Dick Hoover, Harry Smith, and Billy Welu—all opted for the PBA and the glory of individual performance in the professional game.

In more recent years, the ABC conducted the World Team Challenge. Regional tournaments were conducted throughout the country to qualify winners who competed against one another in a championship at the end of the year. Unfortunately, the World Team Challenge came to an end. The format in the finals was based on the Baker system of scoring, designed by Frank Baker, the late executive secretary of the ABC. Baker originated this scoring method for FIQ (Fédération Internationale des Quilleurs, or International Bowling Federation) tournaments.

The Baker system puts greater emphasis on the team concept and practically eliminates individualism in the sport. Each bowler bowls one frame, with the leadoff player bowling the 1st and 5th frames, the second bowler the 2nd and 6th, and so on. The anchor has the opportunity to bowl two additional frames (the 11th and 12th), providing that he or she strikes in the 10th. The Baker system is widely employed in collegiate bowling and in most team FIQ international play.

Open Play

Open play can consist of either organized or unorganized games. Organized open play includes activities such as birthday parties, company outings, glow bowling, or rock 'n' roll bowling. Unorganized open play might involve friends rolling a couple of games on the spur of the moment, children going out with their parents, or couples bowling on a date. It might also mean someone going out to practice, whether alone, with a coach, or with one or two others who can offer analysis and critique. Unfortunately, bowlers are subject to the old adage, "Too many cooks spoil the broth," so if you do practice with friends you must take advice only from those who know your bowling style and are competent bowlers or coaches and thus know the game. Like many other individual sports, bowling is replete with wannabe coaches whose comments are well-meaning but unfounded. Although practice is the key to improving and advancing your game to another level, it is beneficial only when done properly.

Tournament Bowling

Tournament bowling is a more organized activity, where competition is at its fiercest. These events can take place in a day or over a weekend, a month, or several months. They range from in-center competitions to city, state, regional, national, and international championships where medals are awarded. People place equal importance on the yearly city and state tournaments that determine champions in all categories. The most significant nonprofessional tournaments in the United States are the annual ABC and WIBC Championships. These contests, reserved for amateurs, are used to determine the top performers in team, doubles, singles, and all events. They are held at the National Bowling Stadium in Reno every third year; in the other two years, they are held in communities chosen several years in advance.

In the men's division, touring professionals are not permitted to bowl, but regional players and nontouring players can participate in the annual ABC tournament, and each team is permitted two nontouring pros. PBA touring players interested in maintaining an ABC record and establishing an average can do so by performing in the annual ABC Masters Tournament. The WIBC national tournament features four divisions of competition:

Open division: 180 average and over

Division 1: 165 to 179 average

Division 2: 150 to 164 average

Division 3: 149 average and under

In the open division of team play, WIBC rules allow two professionals per team; in doubles, only one pro bowler is permitted.

High School Bowling

One of the greatest motivations for aspiring bowlers is provided by the United States Bowling Congress. The USBC High School program guides all levels of high school bowling, providing rules and instructional opportunities. USBC High School offers a free membership program, and coaches receive resource materials including the USBC Coaches Guidebook and USBC High School Guide, which enables them to nominate outstanding bowlers to the national Dexter/USBC High School All-American Team. It also provides high-score recognition to student-athletes.

Many high schools choose to offer bowling programs because start-up and maintenance costs are relatively low. Bowling gives students a chance to become involved with their school and lays the foundation for lifetime sport activity. It can also help athletes earn scholarships and an opportunity to bowl in college. The USBC High School program is a resource that school administrators, state athletic associations, state bowling proprietor associations, and industry member organizations can use in creating and maintaining high school bowling programs.

Bowling has been the fastest-growing high school sport in the 2000s, according to the newest participation survey by the National Federation of State High School Associations. This is great news for America's bowling youth. Since the 2000–2001 season, bowling participation has more than doubled, and the number of schools participating has nearly tripled.

These figures bode well for the sport of bowling, which has not only attracted thousands of high schoolers but also increased bowling participation on the college level. These developments have proven a blessing for many American youngsters who have no opportunity to gain a letter in other sports because they lack the height, weight, or brawn required for, say, football or basketball.

Collegiate Bowling

Collegiate competition transitions youth bowling athletes into the adult ranks, furthering their lifetime commitment to the sport. USBC Collegiate provides great visibility for the sport by showcasing the best collegiate athletes throughout the nation.

USBC Collegiate is dedicated to providing collegiate bowling opportunities that enhance students' academic, athletic, and personal development. The National Collegiate Athletic Association (NCAA) and the National Junior College Athletic Association (NJCAA) recognize USBC Collegiate as bowling's national intercollegiate governing body. It maintains the eligibility of club and varsity bowling teams through sanctioning, certification, and regulation of the sport at the collegiate level.

USBC Collegiate also oversees and conducts the USBC Intercollegiate Team and Singles Championships and works with the National Collegiate Bowling Coaches Association to determine All-American and Academic All-American recognition, as well as Rookie of the Year and Most Valuable Player honors.

Today, nearly 200 colleges offer intercollegiate bowling programs that compete in more than 60 tournaments annually. These programs include club, NAIA (National Association of Intercollegiate Athletics), NJCAA varsity (men and women), and varsity (women only) teams. Varsity programs operate under rules and regulations of their member athletic organizations.

The USBC intercollegiate program has produced some of the top bowlers in the professional ranks. Here are some notables:

Hillsboro Community College: Tom Crites

Wichita State University: Chris Barnes, Patrick Healey Jr., Justin Hromek, Mike Jasnau, Sean Rash, and Rick Steelsmith

Vincennes University: Billy Oatman

San José State University: Lynda Norry Barnes, Tony Reyes, and Kim Terrell

University of South Carolina: Jeff Bellinger

Saginaw Valley State University: Bill O'Neill and Kurt Pilon

Arizona State University: Joe Ciccone

West Texas State University: Carolyn Dorin-Ballard, Cathy Dorin-Lizzi, Jack Jurek, Marc McDowell, Mark Scroggins, Mike Scroggins, and Tammy Turner

West Texas A&M University: D.J. Archer, Wes Malott, and Karen Stroud

University of Nebraska: Paul Fleming and Shannon Pluhowsky

San Diego State University: Robert Smith

California State University, Fullerton: Missy Bellinder

Morehead State University: Liz Johnson and Kelly Kulick

Solano Community College: Nikki Gianulius

University of Illinois: Michelle Mullen

Elite Bowling

Elite bowling can be broken down into two categories: professional and amateur. A professional either earns a living by performing and competing in the sport or earns as much money in the game as in his or her chosen profession.

Men in the PBA are card-carrying professionals who have declared their status as such. However, numerous bowlers in the United States and around the world prefer to maintain amateur status even though, in reality, they bowl for a living. I refer to these bowlers as *closet professionals*. They qualify for all amateur tournaments, including the BPAA (Bowling Proprietors Association of America), U.S. Open, ABC Masters, all megabucks tournaments, all FIQ tournaments, and a slew of high-paying tournaments around the world that are closed to card-carrying PBA and PWBA players. These amateurs are everpresent at all High Roller and Eliminator tournaments and enter practically all brackets and sweepers. These pro amateurs do not usually win the grand prize, but they do take the bulk of the money in brackets and sweepers.

Many of these so-called amateurs earn as much as any leading professional and much more than most touring pros. Nonetheless, elite bowlers who are not in the pro amateur category enjoy competing for spots on Team USA, which offers USBC members the opportunity to represent their country in international competition.

Sport Bowling and PBA Experience Leagues

The ultimate challenge for competitive amateur bowlers is participation in USBC Sport Bowling and PBA Experience leagues and tournaments. Here is where the boys are separated from the men, and the girls from the women—or better yet, where the line is drawn between bowlers who execute shots with skill and precision and those who thrive on soft conditions. As a matter of fact, bowlers who regard bowling as a sport rather than a form of recreation take pride in posting averages between 190 and 215. On the other hand, bowlers who revel in posting 220 to 250 averages choose to flex their muscles on softer conditions.

One of the most heartening developments in bowling is the upsurge in Sport Bowling and in PBA Experience activity. During the 2006–2007 season, the USBC Sport Bowling program enjoyed explosive growth across the board, due largely to the PBA Experience leagues that allowed Sport Bowling members to compete on the same lane-oil patterns faced by professional bowlers. The number of Sport Bowling members rose 120 percent over the previous season, and Sport Bowling leagues were up 134 percent, while centers holding Sport Bowling events increased 155 percent.

Bowling's equivalent of putting yourself in the shoes of the top athletes is the PBA Experience. PBA Experience leagues offer bowlers the unique chance to compete on the PBA's five different lane-conditioning patterns: Chameleon, Cheetah, Scorpion, Shark, and Viper (see figure 2.1, page 14). These patterns, which vary in oil distance and other characteristics, all comply with USBC Sport Bowling rules for oil application.

When you join a PBA Experience league, your goal will be to tame the five oil patterns, which are also known as the beasts. These wild animals are the same patterns that Patrick Allen, Chris Barnes, Tommy Jones, Pete Weber, Walter Ray Williams, and other pros try to subdue in each of the 16 regular Tour events.

Taming these beasts is hardly an impossible task, given that the USBC and the PBA will take you into the inner circle and discuss the trade secrets with you each week through league handouts, videos featuring the pros, and the Web site bowl.com.

Remember, if you want to compete at the highest level, there is but one avenue—Sport Bowling and PBA Experience conditions!

Bowling's Governing Body

Bowling is the largest organized sport in the world. About 80 million people visit bowling centers yearly, and the unofficial number of organized bowlers is around 5 million. Generally, all organized activities require regulations, and the USBC, the governing body of organized bowling since 1895, is responsible for maintaining the standardization of the game through its specifications for equipment. It also sets rules for the game, offers guidance on rules for leagues and tournaments, and provides a court of appeals to which disputes and rules problems can be referred for review, counsel, and decision. The USBC provides awards in bowling, automatic bonding coverage insurance for more than $175 million every season, sanctioning service to more than 10,000 tournaments every season, and materials essential to every league. Most important, the USBC preserves the integrity of the sport.

Today, bowling is one of America's most popular sports—and one of the most organized. It is recognized by the United States Olympic Committee and as a medal sport at the Pan American Games. Nearly four million adults and youths participate regularly in sanctioned leagues throughout North America. Bowling has also progressed rapidly in Central America, South America, Europe, Asia, and Australia; it is played in more than 80 countries worldwide and is one of the few sports in which grassroots participants can qualify for international competition.

Glossary

approach—Area that begins just behind the lane and goes to the ball return. This is where the bowler stands, sets his or her position, and executes delivery of the ball.

armadillo—Clear plastic device used to determine a bowler's positive axis point. The series of lines on the device is matched to the bowler's initial track. When the device is aligned with the ball track, it points to the bowler's axis point.

arrows—Seven aiming points positioned about 15 feet down the lane. Used as a target to launch a ball toward the pins.

axis of rotation—Measure of the direction of the initial rotation on the ball with respect to the lane; measure of the angle between the initial spin axis and the foul line running across the lane.

axis tilt—Measure of the angle of the initial spin axis in relation to a horizontal plane. The degree of rotational height of the ball at release is relative to being perpendicular to the floor. This angle dictates the style of roll a bowler will have, usually broken down into three categories: 3/4 roll, spinner, or full roller. A full roller has little or no axis tilt, meaning the axis will be close to perpendicular to the floor. For 3/4 roll and spinners, the axis is not perpendicular to the floor but elevated upward.

axis weight—Drilling pattern designed to produce little or no track flare and get the ball into an early roll with little back-end reaction.

back end—Area of the lane closest to the pin deck (about the last 20 to 25 feet, or 6 to 7.5 meters, of the lane). This area of the lane is not oiled, but oil can migrate to the back end through continued use of the lane. The ball will hook in the back end if this area is devoid of oil.

balance hole—Also known as weight hole; extra hole in a ball that is used to get the ball within ABC specifications for imbalance. The maximum allowable diameter is 1 1/4 inches (3.18 centimeters) for ABC and 1 3/8 inches (3.5 centimeters) for PBA.

ball path—Line the ball transverses as it travels down the lane to the pins.

board—Individual strip on the lane that runs the full length of the lane. The lane has 39 boards.

bow tie—The area of tight convergence of the lines of the track flare.

breakpoint—Point down the lane at which the ball changes direction from its original trajectory away from the pins to moving toward the pins. Location of the ball path that is closest to the gutter. Low-RG balls have an earlier breakpoint, and high-RG balls have a later breakpoint.

center of gravity (CG)—The heaviest point on a ball. The true CG is a few hundredths of an inch from the center of the ball, although a line drawn from the actual center of the ball through the CG would extend to the surface of the ball at the CG mark. This intentional imbalance makes the ball tend to curve in the direction of the imbalance.

Christmas tree oiling pattern—Pattern in which oil is applied from gutter to gutter at the foul line but tapers to a point in the middle of the lane about 36 to 40 feet (11 to 12.2 meters) from the foul line, thus creating an oiled shape that resembles a Christmas tree. This oil pattern allows bowlers to play anywhere on the lane.

Computer Aided Tracking System (C.A.T.S.)—Device that measures the position of the ball on the lane at various locations, as well as the angle of travel, the velocity, and the friction.

differential RG—Difference between the value of the high RG axis and the low RG axis in a ball, which determines potential for track flare. The maximum allowable differential RG is 0.08 inch (0.2 centimeter). The higher the differential RG, the more potential there is for track flare.

dots—Markers on the approach used by the bowler to set his or her stance before delivering the ball. Dots on the lane are used as targeting aids.

durometer—Gauge for measuring the hardness of a ball. The ABC requires a minimum hardness of 72; PBA's minimum hardness is 75.

entry angle—Angle at which the ball enters the pins. Also described as the angle of the ball's path to a line that is parallel to the lane.

foul line—Line that determines the beginning of the lane and the gutters. Lights adjacent to the lane indicate if a bowler crosses this line.

full roller—Shot in which the ball tracks between the finger and the thumbhole.

G4—An aggressive reactive coverstock produced by Columbia; also called Superflex II.

gutter—Area of the lane adjacent to the lanes on the left or right. Channels the ball to the pit area behind the pins if the ball leaves the lane.

heads—Front part of the lane; sometimes referred to as the maple part of the lane. Usually oiled to allow the ball to skid.

high RG—Area of the ball's core where most of the mass is distributed the farthest away about a particular rotational axis. Drilling pattern in which the pin is approximately 90 degrees (6 to 6 3/4 inches, or 15.2 to 17.1 centimeters) to the positive axis point (PAP). Initially, the core rotates around its highest RG axis off the bowler's hand. The ball skids farther down the lane before hooking. The pin may be placed close to or in the bowler's track.

hook out—Also called roll out; ball has finished hooking and starts to travel in a straight line.

intermediate RG—Area of the ball's core where most of the mass is neither centered or the farthest away.

launch angle—Angle of the ball's path when the ball is first released to a line parallel to the lane.

leverage—Drilling pattern that produces maximum track flare.

low RG—Area of the ball's core where most of the mass is centered around a particular rotational axis.

mass bias—Difference between the value of the high RG axis and the intermediate RG axis.

mica—Rock material added to bowling balls to pearlize them. Pearlized balls usually skid farther, then snap harder. Some new sizes of mica are being added to balls to affect their performance. For example, mica can help a ball roll more easily and increase the arc at the breakpoint.

midlane—Area of the lane in which the ball generally begins to change direction from the initial launch trajectory.

midline—Horizontal line that extends from the center of the grip at 90 degrees to the grip center line.

midplane—Line (also called the "vertical axis line") that runs vertically through the PAP.

moment of inertia—Resistance to rotational motion; equal to the mass times the distance squared. The farther the mass is from the rotation point, the more difficult it is for the object to rotate or slow down.

no back end—Condition in which, through use of the lane, oil migrates into the back end.

pin deck—Area at the back of the lanes where the pins are positioned.

pin in—Pin and center of gravity are within 1 inch (2.5 centimeters) of each other in a ball.

pin out—Pin and center of gravity are more than 2 inches (5.1 centimeters) from each other in a ball.

positive axis point (PAP)—Point on the ball that initially tends to rotate when the bowler releases the ball. The bowler's style determines the location of the PAP, which is measured from the center of the grip, along the midline, and along the midplane (vertical axis line).

quarter scale—Tool used to lay out a ball. The tool covers a quarter of the ball and has a straight edge with a scale to indicate inches so the span can be measured and marked on the ball.

radius of gyration (RG)—Measurement of the effective weight distribution in a ball, equal to the square root of the moment of inertia divided by the weight. The higher the RG, the more the weight is moved out toward the ball's shell, making it more difficult for the ball to rotate or spin, which in turn delays the hook until farther down the lane. In a low-RG ball, the weight is located closer to the center of the ball, making it rotate more easily and creating an earlier hook.

reverse block oiling pattern—More oil is on the outside boards than on the middle boards, creating a low-scoring condition. Because of the heavy oil, the ball will not hook on the outside boards, but it will hook too much on the middle boards because of the reduced oil there.

rotational axis—Degree of forward position of the rotational axis of the ball relative to the direction of the pins. In the case of a rotational axis of zero degrees, the ball's rotation is in the same orientation as the ball's direction; also described as all forward roll. In the case of a rotational axis of 90 degrees, the ball rotates perpendicular to the ball's direction; also described as all side roll.

side boards—Vertical partitions that separate one lane from another.

spinner—Shot in which the bowler's wrist rotates around the top of the ball at release, causing the ball to spin down the lane, much like a top. The axis is tilted up in the air, and the track is small and far away from the gripping holes. This bowling style helps get the ball down the lane before it hooks.

strong back end—Lane that hooks a lot in the last 20 feet (6 meters).

Superflex—The most aggressive reactive coverstock produced by Columbia.

track flare—Movement of the ball track caused by the differential RG of the ball; increases the friction between the ball and the lane. As the ball rotates and slides down the lane, the area of the ball that comes in contact with the lane forms a line of oil or wear on the ball's surface. This is caused by the migration of the ball's axis in response to the drilling, RG, and differentials of the ball.

tube shot—When the lane has a lot of oil from gutter to gutter but a few boards next to the gutters have less oil, the best way to play this condition is to throw the ball on these drier boards or execute a tube shot, which means all bowlers will play the same area of the lane.

walled condition—Also called "top hat" or "blocked lane"; oil is applied with a light coat on the outside boards (approximately the outside 10 boards) on both sides of the lane, and more oil is applied to the middle of the lane. The "wall" is the area where the oil goes from light to heavy in the middle of the lane. The ball will hook a lot when rolled on the outside drier boards but will hook very little when rolled on the heavy oil in the middle. This condition makes high scores easier to achieve since errant shots can follow the wall to the strike pocket.

Index

Note: The italicized *f* following page numbers refers to figures.

About the Author

John Jowdy is a legend in bowling. He is recognized nationally and internationally as an author, speaker, and top coach of the pros. He has coached more than 100 professionals, and many of the bowlers he's worked with—including David Ozio, Del Warren, Randy Pedersen, Steve Hoskins, and Kent Wagner—won their first titles after working with him.

In honor of his coaching expertise, Jowdy has been inducted into the American Bowling Congress Hall of Fame as well as the Texas Bowling Hall of Fame and San Antonio Bowling Hall of Fame. He is also the only member of the Professional Bowlers Association Hall of Fame who was inducted for coaching. Jowdy has worked with every world-class bowler, including Donna Adamek, Mike Aulby, and Pete Weber.

Jowdy is known for teaching the execution and skill of the game, and he has been called the master of teaching the free armswing. He is also a skilled and prolific writer. He has received numerous writing awards, including the most prestigious awards a bowling writer can receive: the Flowers for the Living Award, the Mort Luby Meritorious Award, and the DBA Humanitarian Award. A former president of the Bowling Writers Association of America, he continues to write a syndicated monthly column that is carried in more than 20 national publications, as well as instructional columns for *Bowling Digest* and *Bowling This Month*. Columbia Industries, for whom Jowdy serves as pro tour consultant, has established an annual college scholarship in his honor.

Jowdy lives in El Cajon, California, with his wife, Brenda.